DATE DUE

Twayne's United States Authors Series

Sylvia E. Bowman, *Editor*

INDIANA UNIVERSITY

John Steinbeck

TUSAS 2
(Revised)

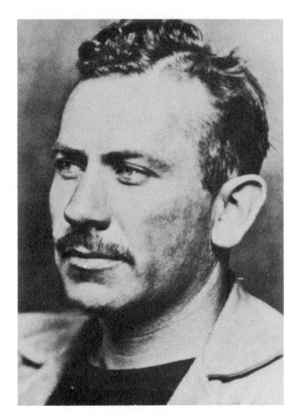

John Steinbeck

JOHN STEINBECK

By WARREN FRENCH

Indiana University–Purdue University at Indianapolis
President, The John Steinbeck Society of America

SECOND EDITION
REVISED

TWAYNE PUBLISHERS
A DIVISION OF G. K. HALL & CO., BOSTON

Library of Congress Cataloging in Publication Data

FRENCH, WARREN G.   1922–
  John Steinbeck.

  (Twayne's United States authors series, TUSAS 2)
  Bibliography: p. 180–84.
    1. Steinbeck, John, 1902–1968—Criticism and inter-
pretation.
PS3537.T3234Z65   1974   813'.5'2   74-16017
ISBN 0-8057-0693-3
ISBN 0-8057-7424-6 (Paperback)

for
TETSUMARO HAYASHI and PRESTON BEYER
in appreciation of their
efforts in organizing and sustaining
The John Steinbeck Society of America and
the *Steinbeck Quarterly*

Contents

About the Author

The original edition of *John Steinbeck* was Warren French's first book and also the first book especially prepared for this now twenty-five-year-old series. This second edition is not simply a revision, but an almost totally new work, developing a new thesis about John Steinbeck's writings. In the quarter century since the inception of the series, Warren French has contributed two more books to it, *Frank Norris* and *J. D. Salinger*; and he is at present completing another on Jack Kerouac. He has also edited more than fifty titles on contemporary American writers, as well as all the books in the Twayne Filmmakers Series.

He has also published *The Social Novel at the End of an Era* (which contains a long section on Steinbeck) and *A Filmguide to "The Grapes of Wrath"* and edited *A Companion to "The Grapes of Wrath."* He has edited collections of original essays on American fiction, poetry, and drama, *The Twenties*, *The Thirties*, *The Forties*, and *The Fifties*, as well as *The South and Film* and (with Walter Kidd) *American Winners of the Nobel Literary Prize*.

A graduate of the University of Pennsylvania with a Ph.D. from the University of Texas, Warren French has taught at state universities in Mississippi, Kentucky, Florida, Kansas, and Missouri, and at Stetson University. Most recently he has been chairman of the English department and director of the Center for American Studies at Indiana University–Purdue University at Indianapolis; but he is retiring in 1986 to devote himself to writing and promoting American studies abroad. He has taught at Dalhousie University in Canada and has recently participated in symposia on American culture at Dubrovnik, Gregynog (Wales), and Budapest. He has received a Doctor of Humane Letters degree from Ohio University, where his books and papers will be archived. Following his retirement, he plans to spend most of his time abroad, with a home base in Swansea, where he is working on further studies of the Beat generation.

Preface to the Second Edition

During the dozen years since the appearance of the original edition of this book as one of the first five publications in a series now numbering over two hundred volumes, John Steinbeck published his last novel (*The Winter of Our Discontent*), his last book (*America and Americans*), became the seventh person of American origin to win the Nobel Prize for literature, and died—after being much honored by his country—at the relatively early age of sixty-six.

This new edition is not just an updating of the earlier one. Only the discussions of what remain Steinbeck's supreme achievements—*The Red Pony, The Grapes of Wrath*, and *Cannery Row*—are basically unaltered, and even these sections have been condensed. The rest of the book not only has been rewritten, but is presented from a new point of view.

In the preface to the original edition, I wrote that my analysis was intended to call attention "to the three general tendencies that have done most to shape" Steinbeck's fiction—"his tendency to write allegorically," "his preoccupation with nonteleological thinking," encouraged by his friend Ed Ricketts, and the resemblance of Steinbeck's "theology" to that of the nineteenth-century American transcendentalists. So much has been written since 1961 about Steinbeck's penchant for allegory and nonteleology that emphasizing these matters once more would tend only further to stereotype thinking about Steinbeck's writing. What is now needed is analysis that relates this work to emerging concerns of literary and social criticism in the 1970s, especially the growing interest in heightening of the consciousness. I have, therefore, omitted from the present discussion most of the material in the earlier book about Steinbeck's allegorizing, nonteleological thinking, and transcendentalist tendencies.

This fresh study might most suitably be titled "Steinbeck and the Drama of Consciousness." Steinbeck's writings have often been discussed as examples of *literary Naturalism*—a term whose critical utility has recently been seriously questioned. Steinbeck's writings have not been considered, however, as examples of what Jerry H. Bryant in *The Open Decision* (1970) calls the *drama of consciousness,* a term adapted from Henry James's Preface to the New York Edition of *Roderick Hudson.* Although Bryant restricts his discussion to novelists who have become prominent since World War II, his key observation that "to be human is to be open to possibilities, to be condemned (as Sartre says) to choose from these possibilities, and to suffer the consequences of those choices" provides a framework for understanding the changes that occurred in Steinbeck's work after World War II as he sought—not always successfully—to present through his allegories a vision almost directly opposite to that underlying his popular fiction of the 1930s. The second chapter of the present edition of this book suggests a way in which Steinbeck's work up to 1945 and his work thereafter may be distinguished from each other, not on the fuzzy basis of their different impacts upon readers, but rather on the basis of the concepts of human destiny that underlie them (though the differences between these concepts surely strongly affect readers' responses to the stories).

By contrasting Donald Pizer's recent speculations on "late nineteenth-century Naturalism" with Bryant's theories, I arrive at what I label a *viable concept of Naturalism,* which I then use to review Steinbeck's fiction in groups that reflect substantial shifts in underlying philosophy and to comment on possible reasons for his uneven success as he abandons Naturalistic writing and strives to create dramas of consciousness. Through this analysis I hope to suggest that Steinbeck's reputation after World War II declined not because he remained frozen in outmoded patterns of thinking—as many writers who became prominent during the years of the Depression did—but because he struggled against great obstacles in his effort to speak with new relevance to an unfamiliar and distasteful postwar world. Once an outraged but sympathetic observer, close to the seemingly hopeless struggles of his subjects, Steinbeck became a remote and often caustic moralist. Such a stance put him at a disadvantage beside younger writers like Norman Mailer, J. D. Salinger and James Purdy, whose relationship to their readers during the period after World

Preface to the Second Edition

War II was like that of Steinbeck to his readers during the 1930s.

Because of the requirement of this series for concise, unified studies and because of the great number and diversity of Steinbeck's writings, this book must be limited almost exclusively to novels and collected short stories. Since Steinbeck's nonfiction books and articles, which are mostly reports of his travels and observations, cannot be examined in terms appropriate to fictional works in which worlds are created, detailed analysis of the author's change, especially in his later years, from novelist into journalist must be deferred.

Elizabeth Otis, Steinbeck's longtime literary agent, has been most gracious in providing helpful information and in correcting the biographical sketch. As agent for the Steinbeck estate, she has also granted permission to use brief quotations from John Steinbeck's works. I wish also to thank my good friends Donald Pease and Richard Astro for reviewing the opening chapters and for making helpful suggestions. I am most grateful to Jacob Steinberg, President of Twayne Publishers, for encouraging me to revamp my earlier study in the light of new insights into Steinbeck's works, and to the remarkable editor Sylvia Bowman for providing the incentive that has spurred my continuing studies of an unflaggingly popular and increasingly respected author, as well as the astute editing that has compelled me to clarify my thinking.

WARREN FRENCH

Cornish Flat, New Hampshire

Acknowledgments

The Viking Press, Inc. (625 Madison Avenue, New York, New York) has granted permission to quote in this book from the following copyrighted works by John Steinbeck:

Bombs Away, copyright 1942 by John Steinbeck, © renewed 1970 by Elaine Steinbeck, John Steinbeck IV, and Thom Steinbeck.

Burning Bright, copyright 1950 by John Steinbeck.

Cannery Row, copyright 1945 by John Steinbeck, © renewed 1973 by Elaine Steinbeck, John Steinbeck IV, and Thom Steinbeck.

Cup of Gold, copyright 1929, © renewed by John Steinbeck.

East of Eden, copyright 1952 by John Steinbeck.

The Forgotten Village, copyright 1941, © renewed 1969 by John Steinbeck.

The Grapes of Wrath, copyright 1939, © renewed 1967 by John Steinbeck.

In Dubious Battle, copyright 1936, © renewed 1964 by John Steinbeck.

Journal of a Novel: The "East of Eden" Letters, copyright 1969 by the Executors of the Estate of John Steinbeck.

The Log from the "Sea of Cortez", copyright 1951 by John Steinbeck, copyright 1941 by John Steinbeck and Edward F. Ricketts, © renewed 1969 by John Steinbeck.

The Long Valley, copyright 1938, © renewed 1966 by John Steinbeck.

The Moon Is Down, copyright 1942 by John Steinbeck, © renewed 1970 by Elaine Steinbeck, John Steinbeck IV, and Thom Steinbeck.

Of Mice and Men, copyright 1937, © renewed 1965 by John Steinbeck.

The Pastures of Heaven, copyright 1932, © renewed 1960 by John Steinbeck.

The Pearl, copyright 1945 by John Steinbeck, © renewed 1960 by John Steinbeck.

The Short Reign of Pippen IV, copyright 1957 by John Steinbeck.

Chronology

1902 John Steinbeck born Salinas, California, February 27.
1919 Graduated from Salinas High School.
1920 Enrolled at Stanford as English major; attended inter-
      mittently.
1925 Left Stanford permanently without degree; visited New
      York, where he worked for the *American* (newspaper).
1929 *Cup of Gold.*
1930 Met Ed Ricketts; married Carol Henning; moved to
      Pacific Grove.
1932 *The Pastures of Heaven.*
1933 *To a God Unknown;* the first two parts of *The Red Pony*
      in *North American Review.*
1934 "The Murder" in O. Henry Prize Stories; mother dies.
1935 *Tortilla Flat* (winner of Commonwealth Club of Califor-
      nia Gold Medal).
1936 *In Dubious Battle;* "The Harvest Gypsies" in *San Fran-
      cisco News;* father dies.
1937 *Of Mice and Men* (novel and play—play version wins
      New York Drama Critics' Circle Award); chosen one
      of the ten outstanding young men of the year; first trip
      to Europe.
1938 *The Long Valley; Their Blood Is Strong.*
1939 *The Grapes of Wrath* (Pulitzer Prize); elected to
      National Institute of Arts and Letters.
1940 Visited Gulf of California with Ed Ricketts; *The Forgot-
      ten Village* filmed in Mexico; film versions of *The
      Grapes of Wrath* and *Of Mice and Men.*
1941 *The Sea of Cortez.*
1942 *Bombs Away; The Moon Is Down;* divorced from Carol
      Henning.
1943 Married Gwyndolen Conger on March 29 in New
      Orleans; visited the European war zone as a correspon-
      dent for the *New York Herald Tribune.*
1944 First son, Thom, born August 2.
1945 *Cannery Row; A Medal for Benny* (film); "The Pearl
      of the World," in *Woman's Home Companion.*

1946 Second son, John IV, born June 12.
1947 *The Pearl* (novel and film); *The Wayward Bus*; trip to Russia with Robert Capa, August-September.
1948 *A Russian Journal*; divorced from Gwyn Conger; Ed Ricketts killed; elected to American Academy of Arts and Letters.
1949 *The Red Pony* (film).
1950 *Burning Bright* (novel and play); *Viva Zapata!* (film); married Elaine Scott, December 29.
1951 *The "Log" from the "Sea of Cortez,"* including an introductory essay, "About Ed Ricketts."
1952 *East of Eden*; reports from Europe for *Collier's*.
1954 *Sweet Thursday*.
1955 *Pipe Dream* (Rodgers and Hammerstein musical based on *Sweet Thursday*); bought house at Sag Harbor.
1957 *The Short Reign of Pippin IV*.
1958 *Once There Was a War* (collection of wartime dispatches).
1960 Three-month tour of United States with poodle Charley, from Labor Day to Thanksgiving.
1961 *The Winter of Our Discontent*.
1962 *Travels with Charley in Search of America*; Nobel Prize for Literature.
1963 Tour of Europe with Edward Albee under Department of State's Cultural Exchange program.
1964 Presented United States Medal of Freedom by President Lyndon B. Johnson.
1965 Began "Letters to Alicia" for *Newsday* in November.
1966 *America and Americans*; The John Steinbeck Society of America organized.
1968 Died in New York City on December 20.
1969 *Journal of a Novel: The "East of Eden" Letters* published.
1974 Steinbeck's boyhood home at Central Avenue and Stone Street, Salinas, California, opened as a museum and restaurant on his 72nd birthday.
1976 *The Acts of King Arthur and His Noble Knights* (uncompleted modernization of Malory's *Morte d'Arthur*).

CHAPTER 1

John Steinbeck, American

A S simply one man among many, John Steinbeck experienced the customary personal triumphs and tragedies—births, marriages, deaths, departures from old homes, and arrivals at new ones. Although these events unquestionably often influenced his vision and provided the material for his fictions, these experiences are not really the business of the reader because they cannot account for the special qualities of the creative writer. Rather, it is the special vision that guides the transformation of chronicles of the real world into fictions that we must seek to understand in order to appreciate the career of a writer, especially an uneven and unpredictable writer such as John Steinbeck, who produced some novels that the public received with almost unparalleled enthusiasm and others that it almost unanimously disdained.

We do not know what decisive experience determined Steinbeck to be a writer rather than something else. Although he has given us no personal equivalent of Walt Whitman's "Out of the Cradle Endlessly Rocking," the boy Jody in *The Red Pony,* who dreams of finding a new way to lead the people, just as his grandfather had led them across the prairies, seems almost surely an evocation of Steinbeck himself during the years that shaped his character. We do know, however, that this extraordinary person—one of the very few to both write best-selling books and win a Nobel Prize for literature—had at least two experiences that enormously influenced the shaping of the vision that informed his public career.

The later of these "conversions" Steinbeck himself describes in "The Making of a New Yorker," his most revealing autobiographical essay. (The much longer *Journal of a Novel* tells much about his day-to-day carpentering but surprisingly little about his imaginative powers.) He recalls the day that New York's Third Avenue was piled with old snow when he sud-

denly discovered himself no longer a stranger in the big city
but one who belonged there. The earlier experience we know
of only through an embarrassed but self-confident letter to
his agents and publishers announcing that he had had to abandon the first completed version of the novel that was to become
The Grapes of Wrath because it wasn't "honest."[1]

Curiously, the second event countered the effects of the
first one. The illumination that led Steinbeck to transform what
he makes sound like a biting political satire into a mystical
vision of the oneness of people persisted through *Cannery
Row* (1945), his last "Californian" book and one written
immediately before his final commitment to New York City.
Thereafter, his work became increasingly abstract or journalistic; he lost his early gift of fusing vividly striking realities
with intellectual patterns. Though John Steinbeck came to
prefer to work in New York City, he did not do his most memorable work there. The reasons for this paradox will probably
always elude final explanations, but consideration of them is
essential to a just appraisal of the artist's remarkable but erratic
achievement.

Steinbeck's life spanned exactly two-thirds of the century
that saw Americans change from horse-drawn provincials to
jet-propelled megapolitans; that saw the United States change
from a great mecca for immigrants seeking freedom and personal dignity to an exclusionist country—a closed corporation
with limited preference for the kindred of the earliest share-
holders; and that also saw this country change from a sanctuary
rigidly isolated from international power politics to a self-
appointed world policeman hopelessly bogged down in a
thankless struggle in a remote area of the world.

The pattern of Steinbeck's life followed remarkably closely
the most typical American pattern of his era. Born in a tranquil,
narrowly moralistic rural community, he left the countryside
to go to college and then try his luck in the big city. His
election of a writing career was not entirely characteristic
(though far from aberrant), but his initial disgruntlement with
the "big town" was characteristic of the "Waste Land" years.
Achieving at last success beyond anything he imagined or
feared, he migrated permanently to America's biggest city and
became a kind of citizen of the world, ending his days as
a counselor to the mighty. Who might be better equipped by

experience to chronicle the American dream as it sometimes turned nightmare?

Yet Steinbeck—unlike his towering contemporary, Thomas Wolfe, whose career followed a similar course until its lamentably early end—did not build his reputation on a direct transformation of his private experience into myth. An extremely private person—like many recent novelists—until near the end of his life, Steinbeck based his stories on his observations rather than on his personal crises, granted few interviews, and rarely appeared publicly. Although he wrote best about the places and persons he had know longest and best, he reserved for himself the role of quiet moralist. After winning the Nobel Prize, he was asked (during one of the few interviews in which he discussed literature) what he thought to be the major function of a present-day artist. He replied, "Criticism, I should think."[2]

Yet, as this predilection for criticism suggests, encased within every artist is a political man. As W. H. Auden has wryly observed, "The ideal audience that the poet imagines consists of the beautiful women who go to bed with him, the powerful who invite him to dinner and tell him secrets of state, and his fellow-poets. The actual audience he gets consists of myopic schoolteachers, pimply young men who eat in cafeterias, and his fellow-poets."[3] Steinbeck belied Auden's irony, though not to his artistic advantage. Paradoxically, the very private vision that enabled Steinbeck to transcend his earlier work in *The Grapes of Wrath* won him powerful friends as well as powerful enemies and allowed the political man within him to emerge to instruct the world directly through his journalism. As he became increasingly celebrated, he became increasingly withdrawn from ordinary Americans and their problems, as he acknowledges when he writes in *Travels with Charley*, "I had not felt the country for twenty-five years."

Steinbeck's undeniable "decline" as an artist almost surely resulted from a confusion of the multiple forms that "criticism" may take. The journalist deplores, or more rarely commends, specific present actions. The artist, however, is not a reporter, but a magician who conjures up a new world that provides us with a perspective for examining ours. A serious artist is not a tactical, but a strategic, critic; he is concerned not with specific happenings but with universal tendencies. This kind of artist Steinbeck was when he wrote in *Cannery Row*, "What can it profit a man to gain the whole world and to come to his property with a gastric ulcer, a blown prostate, and bifocals?"

But the artist is also not just a philosopher. If he generalizes too much, readers no longer recognize the individual behind the type. We do not know the individual Steinbeck skewers in *Cannery Row*, but we recognize the type. Later his characters become too individual and untypical, as in *Sweet Thursday*, or too general to be recognizable, as in *Burning Bright*. *East of Eden*, like Aldous Huxley's *After Many a Summer Dies the Swan*, vacillates disastrously between personal reporting and disembodied philosophizing. Steinbeck did his best work when he lived close to his characters; after moving to New York he was—like the hero of his first published novel—"split up" by civilization.

I *John Steinbeck, Californian*

John Ernst Steinbeck, Jr., was born February 27, 1902, in the agricultural trading center of Salinas, in a Northern Central California valley of the same name—one about two-thirds of the way from Los Angeles to San Francisco on the major highway closest to the Pacific coast. The valley, famed for truck farming, is especially known for its lettuce and its broccoli.

A powerful root of Steinbeck's inspirational vision rests—fittingly for a writer who has made such effective use of Christian allusions—in the Holy Land, to which the figure of prophetic stature in Steinbeck's immediate background, his paternal grandmother's father, took his family from Leominster, Massachusetts, in the 1840s. Steinbeck writes with great admiration in *America and Americans* and in one of his "Letters to Alicia" of this farmer-ancestor named Dickson (or Dixon) who had been moved to convert the Jews to Christianity by teaching them agriculture.[4]

In Jerusalem, two of the Dixon daughters met and married two brothers from near Düsseldorf, Germany, who were visiting their sister and her husband, Lutheran missionaries. One brother was John Adolph Grosssteinbeck, John Steinbeck's grandfather, who brought his bride to the United States. After first settling in New Jersey, the couple moved to Florida, where the novelist's father, John Ernst Steinbeck, was born at St. Augustine. After being drafted into the Confederate Army during the Civil War, John Adolph moved back to his wife's native Massachusetts and finally to Hollister, California, where he became a prosperous miller. Steinbeck's father followed the same trade and also served for eleven years as Monterey County Treasurer. In 1890, he married Olive Hamilton, the daughter of Samuel and Elizabeth, who had left Ulster (Northern Ireland) to settle in California in the 1850s. (The history of the Hamilton family, identified by their proper names, makes up a large part of the action of *East of Eden*.) Before marrying, Olive had taught school in several places, including the then isolated Big Sur, which was later to become Henry Miller's playground. John, the couple's third child, was the only son; his three sisters were named Esther, Elizabeth, and Mary.[5]

The boy became an avid reader, especially of the Bible, Milton's *Paradise Lost*, Dostoevsky, Flaubert, George Eliot, and Thomas Hardy (particularly *The Return of the Native*); but his favorite work was Malory's *Morte d'Arthur*. This work influenced him all his life, and he worked at rendering it into a modern version. He contributed to the Salinas high-school newspaper, played on the baseball team, and served as president of the senior class of 1919. He enrolled at Stanford University as an English major, but left without a degree after attending classes off and on between 1920 and 1925, including a summer session in 1923 at Monterey's Hopkins Marine Station. Between periods in Palo Alto, he earned money at odd jobs. He also contributed light pieces to campus periodicals and was especially influenced by a creative writing teacher, Edith Ronald Mirrielees, for whose *Story Writing* Steinbeck provided a preface in 1962.

At the height of the "Big Boom" in November, 1925, Steinbeck followed the crowd to New York City, where a brother-in-law helped him get a job as a laborer on the new Madison Square Garden (since replaced by a post-World-War-II structure). In "The Making of a New Yorker," Steinbeck explains that a rich uncle came to town and helped him land a job at twenty-five dollars a week on the old New York *American*. He describes his lack of distinction as a reporter: "They gave me stories to cover in Queens and Brooklyn and I would get lost and spend hours trying to find my way back. I couldn't learn to steal a picture from a desk when a family refused to be photographed and I invariably got emotionally involved and tried to kill the whole story to save the subject."[6] He balked at a girl's suggestion that he go into advertising, but he prepared, at the behest of an editor, a collection of short stories for the Robert McBride Company. When this work was rejected, he returned to California by working his way as a deckhand on a ship that went through the Panama Canal. Finally, he settled down as a caretaker at an isolated Lake Tahoe resort to work on his fiction.

After writing three novels that have never been published, Steinbeck finally placed *Cup of Gold*—a pseudo-epic about a "lost generation" version of a famous Caribbean pirate—with the company that had rejected his short stories. He made little from this breakthrough, however, for the novel appeared just two months before the stock market crash of 1929; and by 1936, when the novel was reissued, it had sold only 1,533 copies.[7]

With the publication of a second novel, *The Pastures of Heaven* (1932), Steinbeck turned to the California settings that he was to employ almost exclusively for the next two decades. This novel had actually been started after the third to be published, *To a God Unknown* (1933), a work that had undergone many revisions and that he was still reworking at the time he seemed to have established a connection with a publisher. This publishing house, and even its successor, were forced out of business, however, before the copies of *The Pastures of Heaven* were even bound. Yet, despite the book's troubles, it earned the author four hundred dollars—more than either *Cup of Gold* or *To a God Unknown*, which failed to repay even the publishers' two-hundred-and-fifty dollar advances.

Between the publication of his first two novels, Steinbeck had three other experiences that greatly shaped his life. He was married for the first time, in 1930, to Carol Henning of San Jose, who joined him while he was working in the Los Angeles area. That same year he met Ed Ricketts, who remained Steinbeck's closest friend and advisor until Ricketts's accidental death in 1948. In "About Ed Ricketts," Steinbeck fosters the legend that they met in a dentist's waiting room; but intimates insist that they actually met at a mutual friend's party. Also in 1931, through a woman who wrote Western stories under the name of John Breck, Steinbeck was introduced to the firm of McIntosh and Otis, the New York literary agents who represented him for the rest of his life.

The dozen years of Steinbeck's first marriage saw him develop from the obscure author of some puzzling and little noted novels to one of the most acclaimed writers in the world. The first years of marriage, however, suggested little of this future promise. The newlyweds moved to the quiet, respectable Methodist seaside encampment of Pacific Grove, the particular butt of Steinbeck's ridicule from *To a God Unknown* to *Sweet Thursday*. His family provided him with a small house and twenty-five dollars a month—enough to exist on during the Depression. The young Steinbecks moved briefly back to the Los Angeles area in 1932, but they returned to the Monterey Peninsula before the publication of *To a God Unknown* in 1933. When Steinbeck's mother died after a long and painful illness in 1934, her son's only consolation during this dark period was the acceptance of the first two parts of *The Red Pony* and two other stories by the *North American Review*, and the selection of one of the stories, "The Murder," for the O. Henry Prize Stories volume in 1934.

The precipitous rise to fame, which made a writer who once hoped for an audience of about twenty thousand into the idol of millions, began with the publication of *Tortilla Flat*, a pseudo-Arthurian glorification of Monterey's Mexican-American *paisanos* that Steinbeck looked upon as a relaxation from his taxing labors on *To a God Unknown*. Several publishers rejected the episodic tale as too frivolous for trying times; but Steinbeck's fortunes changed when an astute Chicago bookman, Ben Abramson, insisted that Pascal Covici read *The Pastures of Heaven* and *To a God Unknown*. When Covici became enthusiastic and called Steinbeck's agents to ask about other works, he was sent the *Tortilla Flat* manuscript, which was published under the Covici, Friede imprint. Steinbeck had found the editor-publisher who was to sponsor all of his works until Covici's death in 1964.

Although socially conscious critics attacked *Tortilla Flat* as a sentimental defense of vagabondage, readers liked it, as they did James Thurber's *My Life and Hard Times* and Kaufman and Hart's play *You Can't Take It With You*; for all three folklike comedies consoled impoverished audiences with the welcome message that money wasn't everything. Steinbeck's novel won the annual Gold Medal of the Commonwealth Club of California for the best work by a native of the state, but this award made him uneasy about the effect of publicity. He hoped it might be his last such prize, and he did not attend the award dinner. He also saw his way of life changing when he was paid three thousand dollars—the most money he had ever earned in a lump sum—for the film rights. (These rights changed hands several times, and a mangled film version did not finally appear until 1942, after the success of the film versions of *The Grapes of Wrath* and *Of Mice and Men*.) He made a long-planned trip to Mexico, but he found that he could not work there and returned to a secluded new home in Los Gatos, in the hills of a wine country just outside his wife's hometown of San Jose.

He had little time to brood, however, for 1936—the year that his father died—was one of his busiest. Covici, Friede published *In Dubious Battle*, a novel about a strike that Steinbeck predicted would become the center of a critical controversy. (Party-line Communists did protest his treatment of the labor organizers.) He had to rewrite his first play-novelette, *Of Mice and Men*, when a dog chewed up the original draft. The seed for *The Grapes of Wrath* was sown when Steinbeck visited the migrant workers' camps in order to prepare a series of articles, "The Harvest Gypsies," for the *San Francisco News*. (These were later collected and published with additional material as *Their Blood Is Strong*.)

Steinbeck's reputation soared in 1937 when *Of Mice and Men* was accorded the best reception received by any of his works to that time, despite his own misgivings about the success of the work as a realization of his intentions. Its selection by the Book-of-the-Month Club meant an immediate sale of ten thousand copies, and Steinbeck found himself designated one of the Ten Outstanding Young Men of the Year. He returned in triumph to a New York that he had left feeling rejected just a decade earlier. After touring England, Ireland, Sweden, and Russia during his first trip to Europe, he returned in the autumn to Bucks County, Pennsylvania—which was just then becoming a fashionable retreat—to work on the script of the play version of *Of Mice and Men* with famous play-doctor George S. Kaufman at Kaufman's home. The play, which had already been performed directly from the novel by the Theatre

Union in San Francisco from May 21 to July 31, 1937, opened to laudatory reviews on Broadway during the Thanksgiving season; but Steinbeck never saw the New York production, since he was traveling back to California for another look at the migrant camps. Although the play lost the Pulitzer Prize to Thornton Wilder's experimental *Our Town*, it won the New York Drama Critics' Circle's award on the first ballot and enjoyed a long run before being made into a then quite daring film starring Burgess Meredith, Betty Field, and Lon Chaney, Jr. Yet Steinbeck's name had not acquired box-office magic; for a vulgar dramatization of *Tortilla Flat* by Jack Kirkland, who was looking for a successor to his long-running dramatization of Erskine Caldwell's *Tobacco Road*, flopped within a week.

Steinbeck rejected an offer from *Life* to do a series about the migrant workers because he did not wish to profit from their misfortunes; but he was unable to avoid making a fortune and acquiring international celebrity from his angry and compassionate novel about them. Steinbeck's success came, however, too late to stave off disaster for his publisher; for, in August, 1938, while *The Long Valley*—the collection of short stories that Steinbeck had long wanted to see published—was in proof and while the author was struggling to create his greatest success, creditors took over the house of Covici, Friede. Steinbeck and his editor did not part company, however, for the novelist chose to follow his discoverer when he became an executive editor for the Viking Press. *The Long Valley* was the first of many Steinbeck novels and nonfictional works to bear the imprint of the firm with which he remained associated until his death.

Viking discovered in 1939 what an asset it had acquired; for, had it not been for the sensational reception a few years earlier of Margaret Mitchell's *Gone with the Wind*, the publication of *The Grapes of Wrath* would have been the most remarkable debut of a novel between the two world wars. Although critics and public generally missed the subtle point of a book that was most often compared to *Uncle Tom's Cabin* as social propaganda, they bought printing after printing; indeed, *Publishers' Weekly* listed the novel as the top seller of 1939 and as the eighth best one of 1940. Frank Luther Mott estimates in *Golden Multitudes* that over half a million copies were

sold of the original edition. Steinbeck won the Pulitzer Prize
for the best novel of the year, along with an American Book-
sellers' Award (a predecessor of the National Book Awards);
and, less than a month after the first announcement of the
novel on December 31, 1938, Steinbeck was received into
the prestigious National Institute of Arts and Letters—along
with William Faulkner—on January 18, 1939.

No public disclosures have been made about the novel's
earnings; but, since its publication on March 14, 1939, there
have been a number of American editions, many foreign editions and translations, and a variety of adaptations. Twentieth-
Century-Fox paid $75,000 for the screen rights alone—a record
for the time. Steinbeck's income is also suggested by the
reported $220,000 settlement that his wife Carol received at
the time of their divorce in 1942. Steinbeck had become
affluent enough to make the generous gesture of giving his
thousand-dollar Pulitzer Prize to Richard Lovejoy, a Monterey
department store executive who died in 1954, to start this
friend on a literary career.

Steinbeck also became a confidant of the mighty. Mrs.
Eleanor Roosevelt praised *The Grapes of Wrath* in her column
"My Day," and President Roosevelt invited the novelist to
make his first call at the White House. Steinbeck reminisced
years later in an article for *Collier's* about proposing a plan
for harassing the Nazis with counterfeit money that delighted
the President, but shocked Secretary of the Treasury Henry
Morgenthau. Steinbeck still sought, however, to avoid the spot-
light. Late in 1939 he went with Ed Ricketts on an expedition
to the coast north of San Francisco to collect specimens of
marine invertebrates. Between March 11 and April 20, 1940,
he and his wife accompanied Ricketts on a similar but more
elaborate expedition on the purse seiner *Western Flyer* to the
Gulf of California, a trip described in the "Log" from *The
Sea of Cortez*, which also contains many reflections on the
nonteleological thinking that attracted both Steinbeck and
Ricketts.

Steinbeck had also become interested in the kind of
documentary films made by Pare Lorentz (who filmed *The
Plow That Broke the Plains* and *The River* for government
reconstruction agencies during the Depression). Deeply
moved by Herbert Kline's film about the invasion of Poland

(*Lights Out in Europe*), Steinbeck rejected an offer to work on a film for Twentieth-Century-Fox to travel with Kline to Mexico during the spring and summer of 1940 in order to become acquainted with the nation's remote mountain villages and to prepare the script for *The Forgotten Village*, a feature-length, pseudodocumentary that subsequently won a first prize at the World Film Festival in Brussels in 1947.[8]

Although Steinbeck intermittently lived in California during the 1940s, he was never again so exclusively associated with his native state as during the strife-torn thirties. This decade saw him rapidly mature as an artist until he produced *The Grapes of Wrath*, the masterpiece that was to be hailed in both book and film versions as one of the most outstanding examples of the significant trends in the novel and in films during the first four decades of this century. Though the novel and film found him friends and fans throughout the world, they alienated him from many of the rural Californians among whom he had grown up and who now responded to his treachery with now-forgotten fictional and nonfictional efforts to refute the story that he told.[9] Like Thomas Wolfe, Steinbeck learned that when a writer becomes the dispassionate observer and reporter of his home country, he "can't go home again."

II *John Steinbeck, New Yorker*

"Once you have lived in New York and it has become your home, no place else is good enough," John Steinbeck observed in 1953; but his conversion from Californian to New Yorker did not occur overnight. Steinbeck was restless during World War II. In 1942, he visited Army Air Force training camps to gather material for *Bombs Away*, a propaganda effort to sell still dubious, earthbound Americans on the importance to victory of our growing bombing force. Meanwhile, the author had already made a major fictional contribution to the war effort through the controversial play-novelette *The Moon Is Down*, which reached Broadway in April, 1942, only a few months after the United States entered the war. Although King Haakon of Norway subsequently decorated Steinbeck with a Liberty Cross for the contribution of this work to the liberation movement, its cool intellectualism won it no awards at the time of overheated passions when it first appeared.

Even though admirers of *The Grapes of Wrath* were disappointed with *The Moon Is Down*, Twentieth-Century-Fox paid $300,000 (four times what it had paid for the earlier novel) for the rights to turn the readily adaptable work into an unremarkable picture starring Sir Cedric Hardwicke. (The screen rights to *Bombs Away* also earned a quarter of a million dollars for the Air Forces Aid Society, to which Steinbeck turned over all royalties, though no picture ever emerged.) Far more effective as a cinematic treatment of the problems posed by the war was Alfred Hitchcock's *Lifeboat* (1944), for which Twentieth-Century-Fox commissioned Steinbeck to prepare a script. The novelist, however, denied responsibility for the final plot-line of this controversial allegory, which many critics thought glorified the Nazis too much.

In retrospect, we can see that a major turning point in Steinbeck's career was his decision to acquaint himself firsthand with American fighting forces by spending June to December, 1943, in the European Theatre of Operations as a special correspondent for the *New York Herald Tribune*, then our second most prestigious newspaper. Steinbeck's previous field trips among the Okies and to the Gulf of California had resulted in memorable books, and he apparently had hopes of using his observations in the war zone as the basis for another. But the war disturbed him in a way that even the sufferings of the migrants had not. Though some of the reports (finally collected in 1958 in *Once There Was a War*) have an embryonic fictional form, Peter Lisca reports that Steinbeck was "too disheartened by what he had seen of the war to prolong the experience in any way."[10]

As a result, Steinbeck was forced to backtrack for the first time in his career. Although he produced a "home-front" work in the film *A Medal for Benny* (Paramount, 1945), a tale in the *Tortilla Flat* vein of a corrupt politician's attempt to exploit the family of a Congressional Medal of Honor winner from the wrong side of the tracks, he turned nostalgically for his next major effort to an attempt to recapture in *Cannery Row* the good life with Ed Ricketts in the 1930s. The result was an artistic triumph; but, like many such triumphs—especially some that Steinbeck listed among his favorite readings, *Morte d'Arthur, Paradise Lost, The Return of the Native, A Farewell to Arms*—it was one that summed up a vanished age. Curiously, many of the greatest artists have produced their best work just after the close of the ages that the works epitomize; and Steinbeck belongs to this distinguished chain that stretches back at least to Dante, probably to Petronius, and far into the lost past. *Cannery Row* celebrates a way of life that had disappeared under the impact of world holocaust, just as the sardines had disappeared from the ocean near Monterey, so that now the once busy canneries that have not burned down are traps for tourists who are led there by a novel that they have probably not read.

Even before Steinbeck traveled to the war zone, he had been married a second time on March 29, 1943, to Gwyndolen Conger in a ceremony in the French-Quarter home of New Orleans local-color writer Lyle Saxon, with scientist-writer Paul de Kruif as best man. Although this marriage lasted only five years, it witnessed two of the most consequential changes in the novelist's life: the births of his only children—two sons, Thom, on August 2, 1944, and John IV, on June 12, 1946—and his becoming a New Yorker with the purchase in 1945 of a brownstone house at 175–77 East 78th Street (after having lived on East 51st Street).

Although Steinbeck describes his conversion into an Eastern family man with great affection in his *jeu d'esprit* "The Making of a New Yorker," this change was accompanied by an undeniable deterioration in his imaginative power. *The Pearl* (1947), a Mexican folk story refashioned into a domestic allegory suitable for the *Woman's Home Companion*, has become the special favorite of compilers of high-school literature syllabi; but its characters never manage to transcend a kind of folksy quaintness or to conceal the machinery that moves them. More marionette-show-like is *The Wayward Bus* (also published in 1947), though Steinbeck expressed high hopes for this first postwar exploration of the Californian-American consumer ethos. Even *A Russian Journal*, a skillful account of a trip to America's recent ally in the summer of 1947, with Robert Capa, who provided a distinguished collection of photographs to illustrate the text, failed to interest a public already becoming sensitive to "Cold War" pressures. Indeed, Winston Churchill's warnings of an Iron Curtain descending over Eastern Europe were confirmed by the Russian takeover of Czechoslovakia two months before Steinbeck's book appeared in April 1948. Steinbeck, the man who had awakened the

American conscience to the tribulations of the migrant laborers in the 1930s, no longer had his finger firmly fixed on the frenzied pulse of the paranoid postwar world.

Perhaps 1948 was Steinbeck's most calamitous year, even though he was then elevated—along with Faulkner, Mark Van Doren, and artist Leon Kroll—to the American Academy of Arts and Letters, the fifty-member inner sanctum of the National Institute. His marriage to Gwyn Conger broke up; and his closest friend, Ed Ricketts, died in an accident. Ricketts's death not only severed Steinbeck's last strong tie with California but also deprived him of the benefit of the only severe critic whose judgment he heeded. During this difficult time Steinbeck threw himself into work for mass media; he planned with Robert Capa (later killed on a photographic mission in Viet Nam) to organize a television producing firm. He worked with Lewis Milestone (who had directed the film version of *Of Mice and Men* for Hal Roach) on an adaptation to the screen of *The Red Pony* (1949) that drastically rearranges the incidents but that apparently pleased Steinbeck since the producers (Republic Studios, a casualty of the 1950s) were faithful to his intentions. His best work of this period, in fact, is a script prepared in 1950 for Elia Kazan's film *Viva Zapata!* (released 1952), a tribute to the Mexican revolutionary leader (played by Marlon Brando) and Steinbeck's first historical work since *Cup of Gold.*

The year 1950 brought also the *Burning Bright* debacle, for Steinbeck's third play-novelette was dismissed by literary critics as a well-intentioned but wooden work, one which failed after thirteen performances on Broadway, though it was backed by the usually magic combination of Richard Rodgers and Oscar Hammerstein II. For the only time in his career, a deeply hurt Steinbeck publicly lashed back at his critics with a touching but somewhat beside-the-point defense of his project —"Critics, Critics, Burning Bright" (*Saturday Review*, November 11, 1950).

Scarcely more than a decade after the enormous success of *The Grapes of Wrath*, Steinbeck was being unjustifiably dismissed as one of those "proletarian writers," like Josephine Herbst, Edward Dahlberg (subsequently restored to favor for later work), Dalton Trumbo, and James T. Farrell, whose writings had gone out of fashion with the ending of the Depression by war. Steinbeck's stature in the eyes of the New York Literary Establishment was at just about its lowest point when on December 29, 1950, he married Elaine Scott, the former wife of film star Zachary Scott. This union was to last until the novelist's death, to bring him some of his happiest years (some of them in England), and to see him reestablished as a revered and at times hotly controversial national and international spokesman for American letters and ideals.

Although the couple spent much time abroad, Steinbeck dedicated most of the first year of this new marriage to working in a brownstone house on Manhattan's fashionable upper East Side and in a summer residence on Nantucket Island on a project that had preoccupied him since 1947—a long novel first called "Salinas Valley" that was to become *East of Eden* (1952).

We know more about Steinbeck's thoughts and working habits while he prepared this novel than at any other time in his life because between Monday, January 29, and Thursday, November 1, 1951, he prepared for his daily stint of writing by making entries in a kind of working journal addressed to his editor Pascal Covici which, after both men's deaths, has been published as *Journal of a Novel: The "East of Eden" Letters* (1969). Although Steinbeck felt great affection for *East of Eden* (that he began composing as a letter to his sons) he predicted an unfavorable response to it in a preliminary "dedication" to his editor. "You have written two books and stuck them together," Steinbeck pictures his editor as protesting; but the writer replies, "I have written about one family and used stories about another family as well as counterpoint, as rest, as contrast in pace and color."[11]

Readers and critics failed to accept the writer's arguments and made the anticipated objections that the pastoral story of the Hamiltons—Steinbeck's mother's family—and the contrived allegory of the Trasks never fused. Like some of the involved compositions of Charles Ives, *East of Eden* is a novel that is more satisfactorily explained than experienced. Steinbeck's compositions were becoming intellectual; and intellectual fiction, though admired in Europe, has never attracted American audiences.

This labor of love finished, Steinbeck and Elaine left for Europe and sent reports back to *Collier's* which, like most

popular magazines of the 1930s, was losing its struggle for
a mass audience to television. Steinbeck's first report ("Duel
Without Pistols," August 23, 1952) described an altercation
with Italian Communists—the first of several international
political controversies into which the middle-aged Steinbeck
plunged with gusto; but the series did not become extensive
enough to develop into a projected book. Before *Collier's*
finally ceased publication in 1957, Steinbeck had severed his
ties with it and had become a sporadic contributor of comments
to *Saturday Review.*

After opening the 1952 Venice biennial art exhibition
devoted to American painting, Steinbeck returned to the
United States for the presidential election. Because he was
strongly attracted by Adlai Stevenson's speeches, he not only
became one of their writers, but also provided the introduction
for a published volume of them. After the disappointing outcome of the election, Steinbeck in 1953 visited Ireland—from
which his mother's family had migrated—and he settled down
in Europe for nine months in 1954 and wrote a weekly column
for *Figaro* in Paris. A four-month stay in this city was responsible not only for his much reprinted essay on the menace of
Senator Joseph McCarthy, "How to Tell Good Guys from Bad
Guys," but also for his book that is least known in the United
States, *Un Américain à New York et à Paris* (1956). A series
of impressions of French life and other personal commentaries
that was written in English, it was translated for publication
into French by Jean-Francois Rozan.[12] Although no edition
in English of this collection has appeared, "The Affair at 7,
Rue de M——" was widely anthologized after it was included
in *Prize Stories of 1956: The O. Henry Awards* or as the fourth
and last selection for this annual series of Steinbeck's works.

Other works were less enthusiastically received after *East
of Eden*. Probably Steinbeck's least respected novel is *Sweet
Thursday* (1954), an ill-advised attempt to resurrect the characters and the settings of *Cannery Row*. The two novels provided
material for Rodgers and Hammerstein's musical comedy *Pipe
Dream*, but this production was one of the team's least successful offerings. Another ill-starred theatrical piece, *The Best of
Steinbeck*, died on the road without reaching Broadway. Nor
did the author fare as well on the screen as in the past. Although
Elia Kazan's *East of Eden* (1955) was an enormous success

because it was one of the three starring vehicles of doomed cult-hero James Dean, it was derived from only the last part of the novel and communicated little of Steinbeck's ambitious design. An adaptation of *The Wayward Bus* (1957), starring Jayne Mansfield, attracted little attention; and a very sensitive and lyric variation on the short story "Flight," though filmed by Barnaby Conrad in 1961, has been involved in litigation and has never been released.

Back in the United States in 1955, Steinbeck purchased a summer home at Sag Harbor, Long Island, where he spent many of his happiest days. During the 1956 presidential campaign, Steinbeck again wrote speeches for Adlai Stevenson; and he worked, as he later explained, "not only regarding their political aims but also with a view to making them more understandable to the masses."[13] After Stevenson's defeat, Steinbeck spent much of the next three years in England, where he worked—often with Professor Eugene Vinaver—on his longtime favorite, Malory's *Morte d'Arthur.*

Steinbeck had always been uneasy about writing satire, but in 1957 he produced what is, except for the early "Saint Katy the Virgin," one of his most amusing creations: *The Short Reign of Pippin IV.* A burlesque of the tempestuous French politics and literary fashions of the 1950s, this novel clearly satirizes the American situation during the decade. Even funnier, however, is "How Mr. Hogan Robbed a Bank," a tongue-in-cheek attack on stereotyped American thinking that appeared in the *Atlantic Monthly* (March, 1956). This story also provided a springboard for Steinbeck's last novel *The Winter of Our Discontent* (1961), which was serialized in *McCall's*; but the adroit playfulness of the short story was blunted into heavy-handed moralizing in the longer work.

The 1960s witnessed an amazing rehabilitation of Steinbeck's once fading literary reputation. Disappointed by the failure of Adlai Stevenson's campaign for a third nomination (Steinbeck had served as chairman of an advisory committee that had led a fight against the drift of intellectuals to the support of John Kennedy), he made a tour during the autumn of 1960 to rediscover America; and he chronicled it in the enormously popular *Travels with Charley*—the book that won the author a new generation of readers and that made the elegant, blue French poodle Charley the kind of national institution that the indefatigable turtle in *The Grapes of Wrath* had become.

Steinbeck left again for Europe with his wife and sons in the autumn of 1961 for a ten-month tour. He returned to Sag Harbor in June, 1962, and was living quietly there when one night late in October he heard on television that he had been awarded the Nobel Prize for literature. He had been mentioned for this honor as early as 1945, when it was awarded to the Chilean poetess Gabriela Mistral, and he had remained in contention as the prize had gone to Hemingway and Faulkner. The publication of *The Winter of Our Discontent*—though the novel was indifferently received by American reviewers —provided the Swedish committee with the chance to honor at last John Steinbeck. American response to the award was mixed. Steinbeck himself told reporters that he didn't really think he deserved it. Establishment critic Arthur Mizener struck the official pose by asking condescendingly in the *New York Times Book Review* (December 9, 1962) "Does a Moral Vision of the Thirties Deserve a Nobel Prize?" and by arguing that it didn't. Loyal readers, however, were elated; and sales of Steinbeck's writings, especially in new paperback editions attractive to young readers, zoomed upward. The author went to Stockholm to accept the award in December, 1962, and in two paragraphs of his brief acceptance speech he defined as he had nowhere else his concept of the writer:

The ancient commission of the writer has not changed. He is charged with exposing our many grievous faults and failures, with dredging up to the light our dark and dangerous dreams for the purpose of improvement.

Furthermore, the writer is delegated to declare and to celebrate man's proven capacity for greatness of heart and spirit—for gallantry in defeat, for courage, compassion and love. In the endless war against weakness and despair, these are the bright rally flags of hope and of emulation. I hold that a writer who does not passionately believe in the perfectibility of man has no dedication nor any membership in literature.

After emerging belatedly as a cultural ambassador, Steinbeck returned to Europe in autumn, 1963, with Edward Albee to make a nine-week tour of Finland, Russia, Poland, Austria, Hungary, Czechoslovakia, and Germany under the auspices of the Department of State's Cultural Exchange program.

In 1964, Steinbeck campaigned actively for the reelection of his friend President Lyndon B. Johnson and also received still further recognition from the government. On September 14, along with twenty-four other men and five women, he received from President Johnson at a White House ceremony the United States Medal of Freedom. (Other writers honored were T. S. Eliot, Carl Sandburg, and Texas folklorist J. Frank Dobie.) Earlier, in 1963, Steinbeck had been appointed to a three-year term as an honorary consultant in American literature to the Library of Congress, along with Katherine Anne Porter, Saul Bellow, Elmer Rice, and Richard Eberhart.

Following the election, Steinbeck remained one of Johnson's intimate advisors. The Steinbecks and the Billy Grahams, for example, were reported to have spent the weekend of July 17–18, 1965, with the Johnsons at Camp David. Steinbeck had already been appointed in 1964 a trustee of the John F. Kennedy Memorial Library, and in 1966 President Johnson appointed him to replace David Brinkley on the National Arts Council.

In November, 1965, the internationally honored novelist embarked on one of his strangest projects, a series of weekly "Letters to Alicia"—Alicia Paterson Guggenheim, the deceased wife of Harry F. Guggenheim, publisher of the Long Island newspaper *Newsday*, which carried these reports in a special weekend supplement. The reports came first from Sag Harbor, but they began to arrive from Ireland, Israel, and at last Viet Nam. Generally, the letters decried a lack of respect for law and order among American youth. The letters from Viet Nam, which strongly supported President Johnson's increasingly unpopular policies, became especially controversial because they ran counter to the views of almost every other outstanding American writer. They were especially vehemently attacked by Russian poet Yevgeny Yevtushenko, to whom Steinbeck replied by blaming the prolongation of what he considered a nonsensical struggle on the machinations of China's Chairman Mao. Steinbeck's son, John IV, served in Viet Nam and launched his literary career with an account (*In Touch*, 1969) of his military experiences there and in Washington, D.C., that reflected views vastly different from his father's. Friends report, however, that John Steinbeck liked

his son's book very much when he read it a few days before
his own death.

In the same vein as the still uncollected letters to Alicia
is Steinbeck's last major publication, *America and Americans*
(1966), a lavishly illustrated report on the "state of the nation"
that begins testily but ends with the author's avowal of
undiminished faith in the country's future.

John Steinbeck died after a severe coronary attack on
December 20, 1968, shortly after the narrow defeat of the political party that he had vigorously supported since 1952—and
even before his friend Lyndon Johnson left office and the
withdrawal from Viet Nam began. Steinbeck, who had been
failing since Memorial Day, had suffered a temporarily paralyzing stroke in July. At the funeral service, Henry Fonda, who
had played Tom Joad in the film version of *The Grapes of
Wrath*, read Tennyson's poem "Ulysses" and selections from
J. M. Synge and Robert Louis Stevenson, long a particular
favorite of Steinbeck's, whose *Travels with a Donkey* may
have provided an inspiration for *Travels with Charley*. Steinbeck's ashes were buried in Salinas.

Since his death, only *Journal of a Novel* has been published,
although many provocative essays remain uncollected. His
widow is preparing an edition of his letters that will be indispensable to future studies of his life and work; but no biography
has as yet been commissioned. The library in his hometown
bears his name, as does a motion picture theater on Cannery
Row. A number of his works—"The Harness," *The Red Pony,
Of Mice and Men, Travels with Charley, America and
Americans*—have been adapted for television, and he is the
subject of a film circulated abroad by the United States Information Service. His novels—especially from the 1930s—continue
to sell well when most of the proletarian sagas of the period
are forgotten. Many readers at home and abroad have gained
their strongest image of that troubled decade through Steinbeck's vivid fictional portrayal of it. Even Steinbeck's death
came at possibly the most dramatically appropriate moment,
for the passing of the presidency from Lyndon Johnson to
Richard Nixon marked the end of an era of political promise
launched by Franklin D. Roosevelt that had been criticized
and celebrated by no other creative writer as it had by John
Steinbeck.

CHAPTER 2

Naturalism and the Drama
of Consciousness

JOHN Steinbeck is one of the dozen American novelists whose work is analyzed in detail in Charles Child Walcutt's *American Literary Naturalism: A Divided Stream* (1956), and critics have been generally content to classify Steinbeck's work as *Naturalistic*, whatever the term may mean. Since the appearance of Walcutt's book, however, questions have risen about the utility of the term in critical discussions of literature. As a starting point for reviewing this inquiry, we may consider the definition in *The Oxford Companion to American Literature* as reflecting "received opinion": "Naturalism, critical term applied to the method of literary composition that aims at a detached, scientific objectivity in the treatment of natural man.... It conceives of man as controlled by his passions, or by his social and economic environment and circumstances. Since in this view man has no free will, the naturalistic writer does not attempt to make moral judgments, and as a determinist he leans toward pessimism."

I The Problem of Naturalism

Omitted portions of this definition concern the origin of the term; but enough is quoted to indicate that the problem is whether this definition actually applies to any works of literature. Edwin H. Cady thinks not. In *The Light of Common Day: Realism in American Fiction* (1971), Cady expresses the view that the Naturalistic position "reduced" the universe to "a blind flow of mindless, dicey forces." Man, Cady argued, "was reduced to the merest organism, fighting meaninglessly, at the mercy of chance and force to foredoomed loss." Cady regards the Naturalists' position as being that man cannot possibly intellectually or imaginatively control his environment—a position that leads him to observe that "there really are no

naturalists in American literature" because he is not aware
of any work of fiction that will stand adequately and consistently for the Naturalist sensibility.[1] Lillian N. Furst, who has
contributed an account called *Naturalism* to a series of studies
of "the critical idiom," agrees; and she concludes that "fortunately, with rare exceptions, the adherents of naturalism did
not quite practice what they preached, largely, one suspects,
because it proved totally impracticable."[2]

Even Charles Child Walcutt is compelled to concede that
the term *Naturalism* as standardly used in literary criticism
doesn't really apply to any creative works because "a work
that was perfectly controlled by the theory of materialistic
determinism would not be a novel but a report." "The formal
looseness of so much contemporary fiction," he adds later,
"would seem to indicate that naturalism cannot achieve the
coherence and integrity that go with a completely acceptable
criticism of life." Walcutt attempts to salvage the term by arguing that "it is irrelevant to ask" whether a novel like Dreiser's
An American Tragedy is optimistic or pessimistic; "the question is whether it is true." (But truth, we might object, provides
criteria for evaluating reports, not fictions. Fiction may contain
a kind of truth, but it need not be verifiably factual.) He also
maintains that human free will "is not really absent from the
naturalistic novel" but is "taken away from the protagonist
and the other characters and transferred to the reader and
to society at large."[3]

But all novels might be discussed in terms of either characters or readers, and a term that is useful only in discussing
novels as they affect readers could only confuse comparisons
of the form and contents of such novels and others. Walcutt
perceives a quality that distinguishes what may be called
Naturalistic novels from others, but he fails to provide a
method of using the term in making any general classification
of novels from a consistent viewpoint. As Cady argues, for
a term "to have any viable critical use," it must "distinguish
some kind of true, of successful literature from other kinds."
Since *Naturalism* seems to apply only to nonexistent illustra-
tions of a misguided theory, perhaps it should be dropped
from the critical vocabulary.

Donald Pizer, however, has made a powerful effort to retain
the term not as a description for possibly nonexistent illustra-

tions of a preconceived philosophical position but as a label for certain successful works of literature that display demonstrably different qualities from other works. The "modified description" that Pizer advances in "Late Nineteenth-Century Naturalism" must be quoted at length as a springboard for a discussion of *Naturalism* as a useful term in literary criticism:

I suggest that the naturalistic novel usually contains two tensions or contradictions, and that the two in conjunction comprise both an interpretation of experience and a particular aesthetic recreation of experience. In other words, the two constitute the theme and form of the naturalistic novel. The first tension is that between subject matter of the naturalistic novel and the concept of man which emerges from this subject matter. The naturalist populates his novel primarily from the lower middle class or lower class. His characters are the poor, the uneducated, the unsophisticated. . . . The second tension involves the theme of the naturalistic novel. The naturalist often describes his characters as though they are conditioned by environment, heredity, instinct or chance. But he also suggests a compensating humanistic value in his characters or their fates which affirms the significance of the individual and of his life. . . . The naturalistic novel is therefore not so superficial or reductive as it implicitly appears to be in its conventional definition. . . . It suggests that even the least significant human being can feel and strive powerfully and can suffer the extraordinary consequences of his emotions.[4]

The only troublesome things about this key passage in Pizer's well-conceived and generally persuasive theory are his assertion that the Naturalistic novel deals "primarily" with the lower middle class or lower class and his use of the term "least significant human being" because such emphasis risks identifying the "Naturalistic novel" with what is usually labeled the "proletarian novel." The problem about those "conditioned" characters of whom Pizer speaks is not that they lack "significance"—their actions may have calamitous importance—but that, as Walcutt recognizes, they lack control over the consequences of their behavior. The important way in which Pizer answers Cady's objections is by acknowledging that even those who lack such control "can feel and strive powerfully," as well as "suffer" (and make others suffer). Pizer has not sufficiently emphasized, however, that the characters of whom he speaks are represented by their creators as "feeling" rather than "thinking." They are conceived like the young lovers in Frank Norris's *Blix* as having brains "almost as empty of thought or reflection as those of two fine, clean animals."

II *Drama of Consciousness*

Novels that focus on such characters need to be discriminated from those that deal primarily with characters seeking to exercise thoughtful control over situations. Curiously, previous discussions of Naturalism have not settled on a descriptive term for such *non-Naturalistic* works. The term *non-Naturalistic* itself has undesirable supernatural or fantastic connotations. I believe this shortcoming in the critical vocabulary can be remedied by using the term that Jerry H. Bryant adapts for *The Open Decision* (1970) from Henry James's preface to the New York Edition of *Roderick Hudson*—the *drama of consciousness*. That James himself was aware of the distinction between the two kinds of creative intentions that I wish to contrast here—and even felt in some measure Cady's later annoyance—is evident from his statement in an essay on Mrs. Humphry Ward (1892): "Life, for Mrs. Humphry Ward, as the subject of a large canvas, means predominantly the life of the thinking, the life of the sentient creature, whose chronicler at the present hour, so little is he in fashion, it has been almost an originality on her part to become."[5]

The striking distinction between the characters that Theodore Dreiser created for a novel like *Sister Carrie* that Pizer labels Naturalistic and those that James created for *Roderick Hudson*, for example, is that the former are not represented as conscious of what they are doing or as capable of any self-analysis of their motivations, while the James characters are. A useful distinction may be made, therefore, between fictions that deal essentially with characters whose creators represent them as aware of what they are doing and of the potential consequences of these actions and those fictions that deal essentially with characters envisioned by their creators as at the mercy of such forces as "environment, heredity, instinct and chance" (as well as of cynical manipulators and self-appointed messiahs).

Occasionally the paths of these two kinds of characters cross, as in Henry James's "The Real Thing"; but James's interest in that story is in the consciousness of the artist, not the economic salvation of the Monarchs. The illustration demonstrates, however, that while Naturalistic characters are likely to come from the lower classes, they are not found only there. There are poor people who know what they are doing and often even choose poverty over contaminated wealth (Faulkner's Ike McCaslin or Lucas Beauchamp, for example), and there are also characters who are wealthy (though often only temporarily) who literally do not know what they are doing (like Faulkner's Compsons and F. Scott Fitzgerald's Tom and Daisy Buchanan). John Steinbeck captures in a conversation in *Cannery Row* the difference between the rich and the powerful who are driven by blind ambition and those who are poor by choice, not chance. Two men that the world would call wastrels discuss the leader of their band:

> Hazel kicked sand on the fire. "I bet Mack could of been president of the U.S. if he wanted," he said.
> "What could he do with it if he had it?" Jones asked. "There wouldn't be no fun in that."

The distinction can be most precisely established, however, through contemplation of one of the closing passages of *The Red Badge of Courage* in which Stephen Crane observes that Henry Fleming smiled " ... for he saw that the world was a world made for him, though many discovered it to be made of oaths and walking sticks. He had rid himself of the red sickness of battle. ... He had been an animal blistered and sweating in the heat and pain of war. He turned now with a lover's thirst to images of tranquil skies, fresh meadows, cool brooks—an existence of soft eternal peace."

The characters in Naturalistic novels are precisely those —like Crane's characters Maggie and George's mother, as well as Dreiser's Hurstwood—who discover the world to be made of "oaths and walking sticks" and who are at last overwhelmed in their efforts to control their fates. Even Jim Conklin in *The Red Badge of Courage* belongs in this group, as does Henry Fleming himself, as he is presented in the first half of the novel. *The Red Badge of Courage* is a remarkable account of an individual's self-discovery, in which what has here been called a Naturalistic character is depicted transforming himself into the principal actor in a "drama of consciousness" for which he can write the script (as Stephen Dedalus does, for example, in James Joyce's *A Portrait of the Artist as a Young Man*). In the first twelve chapters of Crane's novel, Henry Fleming is a victim not so much of society or an indifferent universe as of his own naïve lack of conscious control over his behavior; in the last twelve chapters he is depicted as the victor over whatever external or internal forces threaten his self-controlled realization of his potential. The turning point occurs in chapter II when Henry realizes that "he could not but know that a defeat for the army this time might mean many favorable things for him." He has learned that rather than passively resigning himself to "oaths and walking-sticks," he can dynamically create and project an image of himself that will empower him to shape events to his own advantage.[6]

Crane provides exactly the terms to distinguish the two kinds of characters. While Frank Norris's McTeague and Dreiser's Carrie are at times lovable, "love" to them is a passionate feeling, never a controlled commitment. They remain victimized animals who see life as a jungle. Lambert Strether, Millie Theale, and the great procession of James's characters, on the other hand, are "lovers" not in the physical sense, but in the sense of those who have a consciousness of the promises of life and who direct their efforts toward deliberately realizing these promises, even if they are not always successful.

Crane's distinction helps us interpret a troublesome description early in *Sister Carrie*. Dreiser observes of his mindlessly happy creation that "Self-interest with her was high, but not strong. It was, nevertheless, her guiding characteristic." What distinction could Dreiser have had in mind by contrasting adjectives that are usually synonymous as descriptions of states of mind unless he wishes to suggest that Carrie has an overwhelming ("high" in the sense of a natural phenomenon like temperature that is not controlled by the individual) animalistic instinct for self-preservation, but not a self-conscious ("strong" in the sense of developed and disciplined by deliberate training) awareness of how to advance her own interests? Such an explanation accounts better than any fears of censorship on Dreiser's part for Carrie's totally passive contribution to her success in attracting Drouet, then Hurstwood, and finally the theatrical director who starts her on the way to stardom. This concept of Carrie also suggests how Dreiser can speak in the final paragraph of the novel of the "blind strivings" of the human heart and argue that Carrie may "dream" such happiness as she may never "feel."

The Naturalistic character lives in a dream-world of intense but vaguely formulated desires. Few of these characters are so lucky as Carrie; most authors feel that they are going to find the world made of "oaths and walking sticks." The lover who finds the world made for him usually does so because he can advance on his own initiative—as Henry Thoreau prescribes in *Walden*—"confidently in the direction of his dreams," understanding both the visionary quality of the dreams and the necessity of controlled action to make them come true. Carrie makes out as well as she does because she is not a real person in an unfeeling world but the fictional creation of an infatuated artist; even Dreiser did not suggest that she might be able to leave her rocking chair behind.

III *Steinbeck's Tranformation*

Even if these distinctions between *Naturalistic novels* and *dramas of consciousness* serve no other purpose, they provide a firmer basis than any so far suggested for perceiving three distinct periods in John Steinbeck's career and even for suggesting specific reasons rooted in his conception of his characters for his "rise," beginning in the early 1930s and culminating in *The Grapes of Wrath* and *Cannery Row*, and his much discussed "decline" after World War II. These periods do, of course, coincide with those of major changes in his personal vision described in the first chapter and with the general sociopolitical conditions in the country that he greatly loved and criticized. The interaction between these forces was probably too complicated for a critic to have the presumption to try to work out the kind of precise pattern of cause and effect that an author may create in a novel. Order in fiction compensates in part for the untidiness of real life.

A problem with Walcutt's concept of Naturalism is that it does not provide any helpful basis for making a distinction of this kind among Steinbeck's works. In fact, Walcutt lumps the books together as Naturalistic, so that acknowledged qualitative differences between them have to be considered in terms not relevant to the development of Walcutt's thesis. I wish to demonstrate, however, that Steinbeck began in the late 1920s—during the "Waste Land" era of prosperity—to write a kind of drama of consciousness quite conventional at that time; that he turned during the Depression of the 1930s to novels focused upon Naturalistic characters as I have described them in this chapter; and that in *The Grapes of Wrath* he then turned what had started to be a Naturalistic novel into a drama of consciousness by tracing the history of characters that he endows with the ability to save themselves morally and spiritually, if not physically, by developing a consciousness in the face of a challenge from forces that it seemed must irresistibly destroy them both physically and spiritually.

Steinbeck's work after *The Grapes of Wrath*, I then argue with the distinctions established in this chapter, is not at all Naturalistic. He devotes himself to the creation of the kind of dramas of consciousness that Jerry H. Bryant argues were being also created by the most significant American novelists who began to write after World War II. Like some of them, however, Steinbeck found it increasingly difficult to create convincingly Realistic fictions to present the generally hopeful outlook underlying his dramas of consciousness. When interviewed after winning the Nobel Prize for literature, Steinbeck observed that it was more difficult to determine in the 1950s and 1960s than it had been in the 1930s who the underdogs were. I argue, however, that he was really no longer concerned after World War II with creating underdogs—except in subsidiary roles—but was engaged rather in the much more difficult task of giving fictional life to what Stephen Crane called "lovers."

CHAPTER 3

Steinbeck Visits the Waste Land

CHARACTERS who provide suitable subjects for "Naturalistic" fiction appear in Steinbeck's two earliest surviving novels. In *Cup of Gold*, William the roadmender—a man of Crane's "oaths and walking sticks"—early tells Henry Morgan that "all the people at London are thieves, dirty thieves." The people of Panama City, who have "grown soft in their security," rush, when threatened by Morgan's invasion of the city, to the churches to confess and kiss relics instead of to the broken walls to mend them and replace rusted cannon.

The mysterious figure of Merlin, after predicting greatness for young Morgan, even generalizes about the character of "natural man" to Morgan's father: "People have so often been hurt and trapped and tortured by ideas and contraptions which they did not understand, that they have come to believe all things passing their understanding are vicious and evil—things to be stamped out and destroyed by the first comer. They only protect themselves, thus, against the ghastly hurts that can come to them for little things grown up" (146–47).[1] Benjamin, one of four brothers in *To a God Unknown*, lives and dies purely by his impulses, chiefly carnal; and an older brother, Thomas, is purely animalistic, though in a gentle way that makes him feel more at home with beasts than with men.

I *Henry Morgan*

But these characters are not the principal objects of the author's scrutiny. Henry Morgan, the pirate-protagonist of *Cup of Gold*, is a completely self-conscious figure; he knows exactly what he wants and quickly masters techniques for getting it by exploiting the vulnerabilities of others. "I work with surprise, sir," he tells an admiral, "when other men use only force" (120). Having resolved to be a buccaneer, Morgan plans carefully; and he rationalizes his antisocial scheming by arguing, "I have been reading of Alexander and Xenophon and Caesar in their wars. And the thought is on me that battle and tactics—that is, successful tactics—are nothing more than a glorified trickery. The force is necessary, and the arms, of course; but the war is really won by the man who sits back, like one cheating at cards, and confounds the enemy with his trickery" (82). This analysis recalls the achievements of Meyer Wolfsheim, the man in Fitzgerald's *The Great Gatsby* who "fixed" the World's Series; indeed, Steinbeck's Morgan has much in common with Gatsby's associates and particularly with Gatsby himself.

Both Morgan and Gatsby are poor sons of "shiftless and unsuccessful farm people" (Fitzgerald's words). Both boys take to sea to make their fortunes. Both get new names: "American Adam" Gatsby invents his—Morgan wins a title. Both are disillusioned when tricked out of great expectations at the end of apprenticeships, and both are resolved never to be duped again. Both seek wealth after being snubbed by fashionable friends, and both are attracted more by the legend than by the person of a reputedly fabulously beautiful woman. They win what they consider their right to her through their achievements on battlefields only to find that the real woman is something vastly different from the figure they had imagined in their dreams.

Here the tales part company. Gatsby remains faithful to his dream to the end and wins Nick Carraway's respect for sacrificing himself to his "grail." But Henry Morgan sells out his dream for personal security and casts his grail on a pile of loot. When Morgan at last faces La Santa Roja, the famed beauty for whom he has sacked the seemingly inviolable city of Panama, which is known as the Cup of Gold, she at first gains the upper hand by taunting him. Taking advantage of his momentary hesitation when he finds her beauty not what he had anticipated, she makes a long sarcastic speech that ends with the thrust that she is disappointed to find him "no realist at all, but only a bungling romancer."

Off-balance because of the staggering blow to his preconceptions and spurred by his jealousy, which is encouraged by

La Santa Roja, Morgan mindlessly kills his only trusted lieutenant. He realizes in time, however, the way that the woman has used him in order to try to protect herself, and he turns the tables on her. When her husband sends an emissary offering to ransom her, Morgan agrees. "I want the money," he tells the messenger, who had "been prepared to think this great man a great idiot." When the woman learns that she must return home, she laments, "You have made me old, Señor. You have pricked the dream on which my heavy spirit floated." She predicts also that Morgan "will turn no more vain dreams into unsatisfactory conquests" (222). She is right; he returns to Jamaica to marry his haughty cousin and become lieutenant-governor after he has scuttled the ships of the other pirates who had helped him make his conquest and abandoned them. Although Morgan did not touch La Santa Roja, he later lies to his respectable new associates by suggesting that his child may inherit her husband's fortune.

Early in this extravaganza, the mysterious Merlin has told Henry, "You are a little boy. You want the moon to drink from as a golden cup; and so it is very likely that you will become a great man—if only you remain a little child. . . . But if one grow to a man's mind, that mind must see that it cannot have the moon and would not want it if it could" (27). While Morgan is hatching the plot to sack Panama, Merlin speculates back in Wales. "So, he has come to be the great man he thought he wanted to be. If this is true, then he is not a man. He is still a little boy and wants the moon. I suppose he is rather unhappy. Those who say children are happy, forget their childhood. I wonder how long he can stave off manhood" (147–48). He can do so only, it turns out, until he decides to abandon his companions and keep all the loot: "I want security and comfort, and I have the power between my hands to take both. It may not be the ideal of youth, but I think it has been the world's practice from the beginning. Luckily, perhaps, the world is not operated by youth" (230).

When two of his former buccaneering associates are brought before him charged with piracy, he sentences them to hang, explaining, "The Henry Morgan you knew is not the Sir Henry Morgan who sentences you to death. I do not kill ferociously any more, but coldly, and because I have to. . . . Civilization will split up a character, and he who refuses to split goes under" (254–55). Morgan has learned the lesson that Nick Carraway learns in *The Great Gatsby* when he asks Gatsby's former associates to the funeral and is greeted only by evasions. Early in the novel, Morgan explains to Merlin his desire to go to sea: "I must go, for it seems that I am cut in half and only one part of me here. The other piece is over the sea, calling and calling me to come and be whole. I love Cambria, and I will come back when I am whole again" (27). But he never comes back; he remains split and secure.

Henry Morgan consciously and ruthlessly exploits others to achieve personal security, but Joseph Wayne in *To a God Unknown* follows exactly the opposite course of consciously sacrificing himself for the benefit of others—yet both men illustrate that Steinbeck did not believe that realizing one's dreams could be reconciled with achieving personal security in the world of the Waste Land, a view shared by most of the Lost Generation writers of the 1920s—not just Fitzgerald, but Hemingway, Sinclair Lewis, and especially Ring Lardner.

II *Joseph Wayne*

From the start of *To a God Unknown*, Joseph Wayne knows exactly what he wants; and he is not swayed from his course by any natural or sentimental force. His first words to his aged father are, "There won't be enough land now, sir," because the third of four brothers is marrying. Joseph cannot be restrained from leaving his father's Vermont farm and establishing himself in the Valley of Our Lady in California. Settled on the West Coast, "All things about him, the soil, the cattle, and the people were fertile, and Joseph was the source, the root of their fertility; his was the motivating lust. He *willed* that all things about him must grow, grow quickly, conceive and multiply" (42—italics mine). He identifies himself with the land and decides he must stay with it—regardless of what happens—to keep it fruitful. He is unmoved by the murder of his lustful younger brother or by the accidental death of his own wife because "a pure true feeling of the difference between pleasure and pain" is denied him. "All things are one," he meditates, "and all a part of me" (113).

When Joseph's narrowly sectarian brother Burton kills the tree in which Joseph believes the spirit of their dead father has taken residence, drought overtakes the once fertile valley. The remaining members of the family decide to drive the cattle to better-watered lands near the ocean, but Joseph cannot leave his land. He solicits the aid of a Roman Catholic priest, who is worried only about Joseph's soul. "To hell with my soul!" Joseph shouts; "I tell you the land is dying. Pray for the land." But suddenly his anger subsides: "I will go now, Father," he says wearily. "I should have known" (310). Following the example of a strange old man whom he had met on a visit to the coast while seeking new pastures, Joseph sacrifices a calf on a mysterious altarlike rock that he has discovered in a grove of pines; but the sacrifice avails nothing.

Then Joseph climbs the rock, takes out his knife, gently cuts opens "the vessels of his wrist," and watches "the bright blood cascading over the moss." The sky grows gray, and the rain comes. "I should have known," Joseph Wayne whispers; "I am the rain.... I am the land.... The grass will grow out of me in a little while" (321–22). While Joseph makes it clear that he does not understand the reasons that he must do the things that he does, he does them with a full consciousness of what he is doing and of what the expected consequences are. In his concern with the "how" rather than the "why" of things, he is one of the first and most completely consistent of Steinbeck's non-teleological thinkers.[2]

Steinbeck does suggest that there is something superhuman about Joseph's extraordinary self-consciousness. Early in the novel Joseph's sister-in-law Rama confides to Joseph's new wife: "I do not know whether there are men born outside humanity, or whether some men are so human as to make others seem unreal. Perhaps a godling lives on earth now and then. Joseph has strength beyond vision of shattering..." (121).

III *Conscious Control*

Conscious control of one's behavior is purchased in both *Cup of Gold* and *To a God Unknown* at a frightening price. The earlier novel concludes with Henry Morgan on his comfortable deathbed, long after he has "split up" before the onslaught of civilization. Like Joseph Wayne, Morgan develops grandiose delusions as he nears death: "I am the center of all things and cannot move. I am heavy as the universe. Perhaps I am the universe" (266). Then in his delirium he is confronted by "strange beings, having the bodies of children, and bulbous, heavy heads, but no faces." He recognizes these as "his deeds and his thoughts which were living with Brother Death"; but Morgan discovers that, if he looks steadily at these faceless things, they disappear; and he amuses himself "by staring first at one and then at another until all of them were gone" (267–68). All that he has done dies with him; all his planning and scheming, deceptions and betrayals leave no lasting mark on the world.

Similarly, while Joseph Wayne comforts himself with the knowledge that his self-sacrifice has brought the rain, the action has no implications for the future. "Thank God this man has no message. Thank God he has no will to be remembered, to be believed in," the Roman Catholic priest observes heretically after Joseph leaves him for the last time, "else there might be a new Christ here in the West" (310). But neither Morgan nor Joseph Wayne leaves a message except insofar as Steinbeck the novelist conveys the message that they have no message and that they have maintained conscious control over their lives and satisfied their ambitions only at the price of severing themselves from all normal feelings and relationships.

"Thomas and Burton are allowed their likes and dislikes," Joseph Wayne muses about his difference from his brothers, "only I am cut off. . . . I can have neither good luck nor bad luck" (113). Consciousness becomes dehumanizing; its revelations are too painful to permit a normal emotional life, a conclusion suggested also by Hemingway's Wasteland stories of the late 1920s. "After such knowledge, what forgiveness?" T. S. Eliot's monologuist asks in "Gerontion." Like Nick Carraway in *The Great Gatsby* , these wanderers in the Waste Land find consciousness a paralyzing force. Frightful as are the consequences of leaving the world in the hands of careless, irresponsible people like Fitzgerald's Buchanans, the writers of the years before the Depression seemed even more fearful of the consequences of too great consciousness. Thoughtlessness produced chaos; too much thought produced the robotized world of Elmer Rice's *The Adding Machine* or of Fritz Lang's film *Metropolis.*

Steinbeck, too, stood paralyzed by the choice between alternatives. *To a God Unknown* implies that the price of too much knowledge and control must be expiatory death; *Cup of Gold* cynically suggests that one survives by surrendering one's dreams. These early novels display none of the passionate belief in the "perfectibility of man" that Steinbeck demanded of the writer years later in his Nobel Prize acceptance speech. His earliest work to be preserved mirrors the sentiments of those young American writers who were taken most seriously in the 1920s. Had he been only a few years older or had he begun to publish a little sooner, he might have been lumped with the fictional chroniclers of the Lost Generation.[3]

Steinbeck escaped such pigeonholing because his early novels are thin works about characters who are too out of the ordinary to provide insight into typical patterns of human experience—works more notable for their elaborate decorativeness of language than for the credibility of the stories. If they are at times obscure, the obscurity results from the portentous presentation of unlikely events rather than from the depth and complexity of the characters' motivations. If Steinbeck had not subsequently written books much more relevant to ordinary human problems, these two novels would surely be forgotten; but, since they are almost the only examples to survive of the writing that he did during the 1920s, they are interesting as the only available evidence of the view of life that undergirded his early fictional efforts and of the closeness of these views to the widely prevalent world-weariness of the Wasteland writers of the period, a group with whom he has rarely been associated. Steinbeck's achievement during the 1930s is even more remarkable than it has often been considered when we look at his powerful accounts of human tribulations from the perspective provided by these cynically despairing early novels.

Further evidence that a then-fashionable cynicism colored his early work is found in one short, uncharacteristic tale that was published much later but that was surely written during this period. "Saint Katy the Virgin," a superficial but extremely craftsmanlike and funny fable, is about an evil pig who at last becomes a saint when her devil is exorcised. The cynically humorous climax comes when two timorous monks who have converted the pig to Christianity bring her home to the monastery. Instead of being complimented, they are tongue-lashed by their superior who tells these "fools": "There are plenty of Christians. This year there's a great shortage of pigs."

Vitriolic satire of conventional religiosity colors all of Stein-

beck's early writing. In *Cup of Gold*, the derision is limited
to caustic comments on the smug Panamanians who rush to
church instead of to the city's defenses to fend off attackers;
but, in *To a God Unknown*, there is unremitting criticism of
the "meager soul" of Joseph's fanatically Methodist brother
Burton, who at last leaves the family to settle in Pacific Grove,
California—a camp-meeting town where Steinbeck lived for
some years and that he treats with a combination of contempt
and outrage from the beginning to the end of his career. Even
the Roman Catholic priest is depicted as failing to understand
Joseph and aid him in his crisis. This anticlerical humor, however, is in the same vein as H. L. Mencken's jibes at William
Jennings Bryan's fundamentalism and Sinclair Lewis's
exposure of Elmer Gantry; and it shows again how Steinbeck
reflected in the 1920s the attitudes of his best-publicized contemporaries.

One more surviving story from this period has been
attributed to Steinbeck. Lawrence W. Jones explains what he
accepts as Steinbeck's debut in a national magazine: "Mr.
Gerry Fitzgerald revealed to Lawrence Clark Powell in a letter
dated March 16, 1938, that Steinbeck's story 'The Gift of Iban'
was published in a magazine he had once edited, *Smoker's
Companion*, under the pseudonym 'John Stern.' Fitzgerald
accepted the story, he said, because it was a 'delightful fantasy,'
and he agreed to the pseudonym because Steinbeck said he
did not like the name of the magazine, and did not want to
be associated with it."[4]

Neither Steinbeck nor his representatives have authen-
ticated this attribution, but there seems no reason to dispute
it. A comparison of a passage from the story with a similar
one from *Cup of Gold* illustrates not only their resemblance,
but also the ornate, affected style of Steinbeck's early novels
that more nearly resembled the writing in the late 1920s of
Carl Van Vechten than of Ernest Hemingway. For example,
La Santa Roja speaks in *Cup of Gold*: "I thought richly of
you once; you grew to be a brazen figure of the night. And
now—I find a babbler, a speaker of sweet, considered words,
and rather clumsy about it." And Cantha, the beloved, speaks
in the "John Stern" short story: "And so I find that I have
been tricked, and your gifts are worthless. I suppose you think
this interminable nonsense you told me this afternoon was
a gift, and it is not even true."

"The Gifts of Iban" (as the story is actually called) was also conceived in the same exotically cynical vein as "Saint Katy the Virgin." In the passage just quoted, Cantha is petulant because Iban has promised her gifts of gold and silver, but these prove to be only the sunlight and the moonlight. The practical young woman is furious and rejects Iban's suit with the observation that "Gold and silver are truly fine things." As the story ends, Iban writhes on the ground, "his face buried in the soft turf." The question of the authorship of this inconsequential fantasy is important only for the reason that, if Steinbeck did indeed write it, it provides the earliest published evidence of an entire consistency in his style and point of view during the late 1920s.

CHAPTER 4

Naturalism—The Story Cycles

I *The Pastures of Heaven* (1932)

T HE *Pastures of Heaven* troubled early Steinbeck critics because they assumed that, since the book appeared before *To a God Unknown*, it was written earlier. Consequently, they could not account for the novelist's reversion to the manner and viewpoint of *Cup of Gold* in his third book after writing a second in the kind of episodic form and compassionate (often even sentimental) manner of such later writings as *Tortilla Flat* and *The Red Pony*. Peter Lisca has established, however, that one version of *To a God Unknown*—and almost certainly not the earliest—was being circulated to publishers even before Steinbeck began work on *The Pastures of Heaven*.[1]

Although the order of composition is established, it is difficult to explain how suddenly Steinbeck, early in 1931, was able to begin moving in a direction counter to that he had followed in any earlier known work. *The Pastures of Heaven* would be a remarkable work for any author at any age; some critics, like Maxwell Geismar, still rank it as Steinbeck's best. Because of the remarkably exact correspondences between the stories and their allegorical burdens, the book operates on several levels without the action's being tenuously protracted to serve the purposes of the allegory—as Howard Levant argues throughout *The Novels of John Steinbeck* it often was in later works. Steinbeck must have experienced early in the 1930s, about the time he had first married and had also met Ed Ricketts, one of those remarkable changes of mind and heart that he describes in his letter about rewriting *The Grapes of Wrath*.

Richard Astro maintains that Ricketts's influence on *The Pas-*

tures of Heaven could only have been "indirect," because "Steinbeck was just coming to understand Ricketts's complicated world-view when the book was written."[2] Yet some powerful force must have influenced the novelist's abandonment of the highly mannered cynicism of his earliest publications for the simply yet poetically expressed despair about the plight of ordinary people that appears in his work beginning with *The Pastures of Heaven* and persists until the opening chapters of *The Grapes of Wrath*. *The Pastures of Heaven* is the earliest work that can be called Naturalistic as this term is specifically narrowed in the second chapter of this book.

Discussion of the book has focused, however, not so much on its style and viewpoint as on its organization, for it is a daring formal experiment for a virtually unknown writer, whose earlier books were conventionally planned novels that suggested little interest in the kind of experimentation in methods of storytelling that had concerned James Joyce and William Faulkner. Argument still continues as to whether *The Pastures of Heaven* is a "novel" at all or simply a loosely related collection of short stories.

Forrest L. Ingram provides in *Representative Short-Story Cycles of the Twentieth Century* a method of settling this debate by considering *The Pastures of Heaven* and other collections of related but individually autonomous stories—like Sherwood Anderson's *Winesburg, Ohio* and Faulkner's *The Unvanquished*—as "short-story cycles." He defines these as sets of "stories linked to each other in such a way as to maintain a balance between the individuality of each of the stories and the necessities of the larger unit."[3] While the stories can stand by themselves, stories in *The Pastures of Heaven* take on additional meaning when they are read in relationship to one another and fitted into the framework that makes this book not just a series of anecdotes about life in a beautiful valley but the ironic history of the valley itself. The one quality that this story-cycle shares with the author's earlier work (as well as with much of his later) is the heavy use of the kind of irony (especially praised by the "New Critics" who rose to prominence in the 1930s) that brings out the differences between characters' great expectations and their frustrating fulfillments.

That the name *The Pastures of Heaven* is ironic is stressed by both a prologue and epilogue that frame the ten tales of valley life. The prologue explains that the valley was named for the impression its unspoiled beauty made around 1776 on a Spanish corporal who was returning to captivity some Indians who had abandoned Christianity and hard labor for a carefree, pagan life. The corporal's dream of spending his last days contentedly in this valley went unfulfilled; he spent them instead locked in a barn where he wasted away with a venereal disease presented him, ironically, by an Indian woman. The defeat of his dream establishes the pattern for the tales constituting the book.

The epilogue is even more heavy-handedly cheerless. Some tourists who peer down into the valley dream about the tranquil life it promises; but the reader knows by this time that appearances are deceiving and that the inviting valley offers—in words that Matthew Arnold had written sixty years earlier when contemplating the equally pleasing prospect of Dover Beach—". . . neither joy, nor love, nor light,/ Nor certitude,/ nor peace, nor help for pain. . . ." Instead, the Pastures of Heaven are the dwelling place of the Munroes.

The Munroe family provides the physical connecting link between the ten tales within the frame; but the book is not so much about them—they are minor characters in all but the first episode—as about their interaction with others. The basic pattern followed in these actions is foreshadowed in a conversation at the end of the second chapter between Bert Munroe and T. B. Allen, the valley storekeeper, which relates the misfortunes that in the past have befallen both the Munroes and the farm that they have bought in the valley:

Bert had been frowning soberly as a new thought began to work in his mind. "I've had a lot of bad luck," he said. "I've been in a lot of businesses and every one turned out bad. When I came down here, I had a kind of idea that I was under a curse. . . . And what do I do? First thing out of the box, I buy a place that's supposed to be under a curse. Well, I just happened to think, maybe my curse and the farm's curse got to fighting and killed each other off. I'm dead certain they've gone anyway."

The men laughed with him. T. B. Allen whacked his hand down on the counter. "That's a good one," he cried. "But here's a better one. Maybe your curse and the farm's curse has mated and gone into a gopher hole like a pair of rattlesnakes. Maybe there'll be a lot of baby curses crawling around the Pastures the first thing we know" (15).[4]

Allen's is the better prediction; Munroe, as usual, is wrong in his dead certainty. Though his personal fortunes flourish after buying the farm that has been a curse to others, the union of his curse with the farm's brings forth a brood of curses for other residents of the valley. The Munroes are never really responsible in any conscious sense for the tragedies they precipitate; they are always well-meaning. Their curse, it soon becomes evident, is that they never know the right thing to say or do; therefore, they have the calamitous effect of upsetting the precariously maintained equilibrium of insecure people. Too uncritical of themselves to recognize their propensity for saying and doing the wrong things, the Munroes constantly push themselves into positions—like Bert's on the school board—in which they can influence the lives of others. Steinbeck launches in this story-cycle the attack on mindless, middle-class ambition that culminates in the denunciations of *Cannery Row*.

The Munroes' pushiness produces these consequences:

(1) The false, but harmless image of affluence that "Shark" Wicks has fostered is shattered by Bert Munroe's hysterically threatening to have Wicks arrested for threatening to kill Bert's son Jimmy, whose attentions to Wicks's daughter the father resents.

(2) The retarded Tularecito has to be sent to an asylum after attacking Bert Munroe for filling in a hole that the boy had been digging to reach his "people"—the gnomes. Bert had jumped to the conclusion that the digging was a prank of his son Manny's.

(3) Mrs. Van Deventer has to dispose of her demented daughter as a result of troubles brought on by Bert's first assuming that he must make an uninvited visit to each new family in the valley and by his then making a thoughtless promise to help the daughter escape confinement.

(4) Mrs. Munroe drives Junius Maltby and his son Robbie back to the city by publicly forcing new clothes on the boy and thereby making the father and son realize for the first time how impoverished they appear in the eyes of "respectable" society. (Steinbeck titled this episode "Nothing

So Monstrous" when it was later published as a separate story.)

(5) Munroe breaks up the Lopez sisters' flourishing business because he thinks it a "good joke" to insinuate to a pathologically possessive woman that her husband plans to run off with one of the jolly girls.

(6) Molly Morgan, popular schoolteacher, runs away from the valley that she loves when she cannot stand to hear Munroe joking about a drunken hired hand who resembles and, she fears, may even be the vanished father that she idolized.

(7) Ray Banks, a man of "meager imagination," who attends executions as a guest of his friend, the warden at San Quentin prison, is intimidated into giving up his trips when Munroe—to cover up his own queasy feelings—tells Banks that, if he "had any imagination," he "wouldn't go up to see some poor devil get killed."

(8) Pat Humbert is inspired with the hope of escaping the blighting burden of his past when he overhears a chance remark of Munroe's daughter expressing interest in his house; but his dreams are crushed when she marries another man.

(9) John Whiteside's hope of continuing a dynasty of rural patriarchs that his father founded is blasted when Munroe's daughter marries his only son and insists on their moving to town to be near her friends. Even his mansion is destroyed by a brush fire started at an inopportune time at Bert Munroe's insistence.

In each episode by thoughtlessly—even if sometimes accidentally—saying or doing a wrong thing, Munroe has destroyed the world that another person has carefully constructed for himself or painfully resigned himself to accepting. The Munroes even destroy the mind of their youngest son by thoughtlessly developing in him such a terror of a necessary adenoidal operation that a hysteria results "that robbed him of his self-control and even of a sense of self-preservation" (12). At one point, Steinbeck even has Mrs. Munroe explain unintentionally and quite self-righteously just what is wrong with the family. Justifying the gift of clothes to young Maltby, she explains that she means only to be "nice" and "kind": "I think his health is more important than his feelings" (86). Since the Munroes lack the ability to empathize, it never occurs to them that other people could feel differently from them—that their guesses about others could be wrong.

Ironically, they destroy their own son's health in a misguided effort to spare his feelings.

Many years later in *Burning Bright*, Steinbeck says of a character who must be eliminated if others are to survive, "Victor's unfortunate choice it was always to mis-see, to mis-hear, to mis-judge." He preaches in this work what he dramatizes through every episode of *The Pastures of Heaven* (the difference in the mode of presentation accounts in part for the enormous superiority of the earlier book). What is said of Victor is shown to be true of the Munroes—as it is true of nearly every "villain" in Steinbeck's works: they do not have the sympathetic ability to get outside themselves. Another horrifying example of this lack of sympathy in *The Pastures of Heaven* is Pat Humbert's aged parents, of whom he reports after their deaths, "They didn't ever ask about the crops, and they hated the rain because of their rheumatism. They just wanted to live. I don't know why" (138). But the Humberts hurt only their own son; when the Munroes' insensitivity to others' feelings is combined with their propensity to meddle in others' affairs, they make an emotional wasteland of the inviting valley.

Steinbeck even carefully plants a clue to his interpretation of the "curse" in the epilogue. A prosperous man, talking about the stone keel of Carmel Mission, explains that the construction is for protection against earthquakes, but that it wouldn't work. A young priest protests, "But it has worked. There have been earthquakes, and the mission still stands" (180). Like the pompous tourist, the Munroes know what will work and what won't; and, like him, they are wrong because facts are a nuisance to them. Because they never bother to find out the truth, they are continually at the mercy of their own erroneous preconceptions. But, because they are complacent about their intellectual and emotional corruption, they are responsible for destroying the dreams of those that they impose themselves upon—and they are culpable not in the insensitive eyes of the law but in the sensitive eyes of the compassionate artist who is distraught that man cannot develop a beauty of life to match that of his surroundings.

The novel is thus much more specifically and bitterly satirical than has usually been recognized; but perhaps the subtle author concealed his intentions too well, for even the recogni-

tion that each episode attests to the same general failing of
the Munroes does not do full justice to the design underlying
the work. There is also a remarkable dramatic buildup through
the story-cycle—like the intensification with each repetition
of the theme of Ravel's "Bolero." The Munroes are not only
at fault in each episode; each error has also more lamentable
consequences than the preceding one. The stories are not
arranged chronologically—Molly Morgan, for example, figures
in some stories before her own arrival in the Pastures of Heaven
is narrated; instead, they are placed according to the gravity
of the offenses the Munroes commit against the dreams of
others.

The first offense against "Shark" Wicks is trivial, and perhaps
his family has even been served well by the destruction of
an illusion that has limited the effectiveness of a man and
that has kept his wife and daughter unhappy. In the second
story, too, although Tularecito's confinement will probably
mean the loss to the world of his talent for drawing, his being
institutionalized is as inevitable and as socially necessary as
Benjy Compson's in Faulkner's *The Sound and the Fury*. Even
if Munroe had not too abruptly precipitated the end of an
idyll, the gnome-boy would at some time either have to be
confined or to be destroyed, like Lennie in *Of Mice and Men*.
Again, in the story of Helen Van Deventer, Munroe does little
more than thoughtlessly hasten the inevitable; but this time
he goes out looking for trouble instead of waiting for it to
come to him. In all three stories, however, if the Munroes
had not hastened the denouements, they would have eventually evolved.

In the next three stories, however, the Munroes are actively
and cruelly responsible for thoughtless actions or remarks that
other people might have avoided and that some others in the
stories do regret. The most ambiguous of the stories is that
of the Maltbys. Although Steinbeck presents father and son
in a favorable light, "public opinion" would probably go along
with the Munroes in trying to do the "decent thing" by clothing
the needy. Besides, the Maltbys can go away and start another
life (as Wicks can in the first story discussed). The Lopez sisters,
however—like Tularecito—are driven from what has always
been their home, not because Bert fancies himself an agent
of virtue, but because what will destroy their happiness is

only a "good joke" to him. In the story of Molly Morgan, his stupid humor also drives away a much more useful and better-liked person than himself—one who was making a positive contribution to the community—just as his stupidity in dealing with the Van Deventers hastens the end of the life of a girl who might have been able to live on harmlessly under restraint.

In the last three stories, the Munroes destroy beyond repair the harmless dreams of persons who cannot hope to make a new start—the first, deliberately; the second, inadvertently; the third, through sheer incompetence (precisely the same pattern established in the two earlier triads of tales). The order in which Steinbeck places his stories suggests that in his eyes it is even worse for one meddling in another's affairs to be acting out of ignorance than to be deliberately trying to save his own face. (The same sentiment is revealed by the author's greater dislike for the owners' paid deputies than for the owners themselves in *In Dubious Battle* and in *The Grapes of Wrath*).

In the story of Ray Banks, Bert Munroe wantonly and quite intentionally sets out to destroy another man's peculiar but socially harmless illusions in order to protect himself from an examination of his own depraved motives and behavior. In the story of Pat Humbert, the Munroes really cannot be faulted; for Mae Munroe is not to blame that Pat's overhearing and making too much of her idle remarks about his house sets him in pursuit of an empty dream. But in this episode and in the final story, we see a new cycle starting. The older Munroes are no longer the major culprits; it is the daughter who insists upon returning to the very place where her parents suffered a sequence of misfortunes because she is bored with the beautiful valley where they have been able at last to flourish. Since Mae has learned nothing from her parents' history, she must repeat it. The story of Pat Humbert shows how disastrous even the idle conversation of such a family can be. Even thoughtlessness can have unexpected dire consequences; and Mae did, after all, want to meddle in someone else's affairs by scheming to get herself into a house that she had been told had been closed to outsiders for years.

The last tale presents fittingly the most profound loss. Richard and John Whiteside have both made great contributions to the valley community and have dreamed its grandest

dreams. Steinbeck writes in this chapter of more than
Whitesides and Munroes; he creates a brief allegory on the
tragic theme of the destruction of the dream of founding a
dynasty that Faulkner treats with somber majesty in *Absalom,
Absalom!*

Mention of Faulkner reminds us also of the way in which
the Munroes function in Steinbeck's work as the Snopeses
do in Faulkner's, but Steinbeck's mischief-makers lack even
the monomaniacal sense of self-importance and the tremendous native talent of Flem Snopes. The Munroes are simply
mediocrities who are complacent about destroying others in
order to preserve their own smug self-esteem. This book
dramatizes Steinbeck's view that the worst people of all are
those who lead what Thoreau called "lives of quiet
desperation"—the unhappy plight of the "Natural man" who
cannot control his behavior because he cannot face examining
it.

II   The Red Pony

The Red Pony may also be described as a "story-cycle"
(perhaps the most perfect illustration of Ingram's terms). Since
the stories now grouped in this work were not collected until
the publication in 1938 of *The Long Valley*, in which the first
three appeared under the collective title; and since the four
were not separately published under this title until 1945, it
may appear unjustified to discuss at this point the collection.
The first two stories, "The Gift" and "The Great Mountains,"
however, had been separately published in the *North American Review* as early as November and December, 1933—the
first of Steinbeck's stories to appear in a prominent national
publication. Although "The Promise" did not appear in
Harper's until October, 1937, and although "The Leader of
the People" did not appear in this country until the publication
in 1938 of *The Long Valley* (it had first been printed in August,
1936, in the British magazine *Argosy*), the stories had probably
been written long before their publication. Peter Lisca reports
that a draft of the final story is found in the same manuscript
book with *Tortilla Flat* and "The Murder" (printed in 1934).[5]
The cycle is also so close to *The Pastures of Heaven* in characterization, tone, and setting that it seems most appropriate
to consider it as intervening between that work and *Tortilla*

Flat, even though the author or publishers may not have conceived of the stories as a cyclical unit until later.

Certainly the most light is shed on Steinbeck's artistic development by considering *The Red Pony,* one of his works in which form and content are most perfectly integrated,[6] as a counterstatement to *The Pastures of Heaven,* as a cycle of stories in which a thoughtless child develops through a series of maturing experiences into a young man who gives promise of leading the kind of "examined life" that even his immediate forebears have not. This story of a young boy's painful but triumphant initiation into the natural world also launches a larger cycle of Naturalistic works continued in the discomforting tales of frustrated young manhood in "Flight," *Tortilla Flat,* and *In Dubious Battle.* There are compelling artistic and philosophical reasons for discussing *The Red Pony* at this point even if there were not abundant evidence to suggest that this arrangement places the work properly in a chronological consideration of Steinbeck's achievement.

While each of the four parts of *The Red Pony* can be read separately and has been individually anthologized, together they tell a tightly knit story of a boy's growth from the selfish ignorance that the Munroes never escape to a compassionate enlightenment as his experiences teach him to see the world not as he wishes it to be, but as it is. The cycle remains, however, "Naturalistic" because we do not see the boy going on to exercise conscious control over his destiny; it is a story of man "enduring" rather than "prevailing."

At the beginning of the first story Jody is a child not only in the sense of being innocent of knowledge of the world but also in the sense of being under others' control. The degree of his dependence is stressed: "It didn't occur to him to disobey the harsh note" of the triangle calling him to breakfast; Jody obeys his father "in everything without questions of any kind"; "Punishment would be prompt both at school and at home" if he lied to get away from school. There are compensations, however, for this dependent status; Jody lives in a world of certainties and believes implicitly in the wisdom of those whom he obeys.

As the story opens, however, Jody feels "an uncertainty in the air, a feeling of change and of loss and of the gain of new and unfamiliar things." The first gain is a red pony that

Jody's father has bought from a bankrupt show. Owning and caring for a pony is Jody's first step toward becoming an adult, toward differentiating him from the mass represented by the boys who enviously admire the pony: "Before today Jody had been a boy, dressed in overalls and a blue shirt—quieter than most, even suspected of being a little cowardly. And now he was different." The other boys realize that Jody has been miraculously lifted out of equality with them; he has been placed over them by becoming a horseman.

With maturity comes disillusionment. The story is built chiefly around ranchhand Billy Buck's promises to Jody. He promises first, when Jody is hesitant about leaving the pony out in the corral on a sunny day during a rainy season, that "it won't rain" and that, if it does, he will bring the pony in. "Billy Buck wasn't wrong about things," Steinbeck comments because, if Jody's faith is to be preserved, "He couldn't be." But this time he is: it does rain, and Billy does not put the pony in but seeks refuge for himself on a neighboring ranch. "You said it wouldn't rain," Jody chides Billy, who replies that it's hard to tell at this time of year. Steinbeck comments, "His excuse was lame. He had no right to be fallible, and he knew it."

The pony does catch cold, but Billy says that "he'll be all right in the morning." He isn't; he grows worse. When his condition becomes serious, Jody asks about it. Billy does not want to tell the truth, but realizes that "he couldn't be wrong three times." Later, when Jody observes that the pony is very sick, Bill thinks a long time about what to say: "He nearly tossed off a careless assurance, but he saved himself in time." Again, though, he cannot save the pony; it flees into a meadow and dies. When buzzards attack the carcass, Jody manages to grab one of them that stares at him "impersonal and unafraid and detached" even as he kills it.

Jody's father angrily asks the boy if he didn't know that the buzzard didn't kill the pony. Jody knows, but he is simply practicing displacement, as he has earlier when he throws a clod at an unoffending but disgustingly healthy dog. He has learned that man cannot always vent his feelings directly on what has hurt him. He has learned also that nature is impersonal, no respecter of human wishes. The most important thing that he has learned, however, is that even those who love us sometimes have only the alternatives of telling us something that we don't want to hear or of lying to us. He can never be a completely naïve or dependent child again.

As the second story, "The Great Mountains," begins, we find that the once-trusting Jody has become cruel and callous. He irrationally tortures a long-suffering dog, and he equally irrationally kills a thrush. When he hides the bird's body to avoid telling the truth, Steinbeck writes: "He didn't care about the bird, or its life, but he knew what the older people would say if they had seen him kill it; he was ashamed of their potential opinion." He is no longer respectful of adults, but he still fears them. He has graduated to that intermediate state between childhood and manhood in which the principal guide to conduct is fear of public opinion, a state beyond which many people, of course, never advance. Like other fearful people, too, Jody has reached a state where he does not wish to accept responsibility. When an old man approaches him, he turns abruptly and runs to the house for help.

This old man is the central figure in the story. He has lived as a child on the land where the ranch stands. He has come home to die now that he is too old to work. Jody's father, who unsympathetically refuses to let him stay, compares him to an old horse "who ought to be shot." Only Jody talks to the old man and learns that he has once visited with his father the great mountains that Jody much admires, but the old man remembers nothing of them except that it was "quiet and nice" there. Jody also learns that the old man's most prized possession is a rapier that he has inherited from his father. The next morning both the old man and the superannuated horse to which Jody's father compared him are gone; they have been seen heading towards the great mountains. Jody discovers that the old man has taken none of his possessions but the rapier. As Jody thinks of the old man, the boy is filled with "a nameless sorrow." This is his recognition that adults, too, are not always to be feared, that they also have their problems, become worn out, useless, unwanted. If youth, as he has learned earlier, has its tragedies, so does old age. His sympathies have been expanded.

"The Promise," the third story, opens with Jody's showing his consciousness of the hurt feelings of the adults he associates with and being treated by them in a more adult manner. His father promises him a colt to replace the red pony if the boy will take a mare to be bred, earn the stud fee, tend the mare until she is ready to deliver (nearly a year), and then train the colt. Jody promises and finds himself "reduced to peonage for the whole late spring and summer." His relationship with adults has subtly changed. Billy Buck will do everything that he can to deliver the colt safely, but "won't promise anything" this time. Jody endures the long wait—the kind of ordeal that a medieval squire would have had to go through as a condition of attaining knighthood. At the end, however, tragedy strikes once more: something goes wrong with the delivery, and Billy has to kill the mare to save the colt. During the tense moments of the delivery, two new things happen: Jody, who used to obey automatically, refuses to do so until sworn at; and Billy Buck for the first time in the story-cycle loses his temper with the boy because of his own frustration at the loss of the mare.

Jody has now irretrievably entered the troublesome realm of adult emotions and defeats. He has learned, furthermore, that just as man is fallible, so is nature. Although the operations of nature continue indifferent to man's wishes, these operations are far from perfect. Nellie has delivered colts successfully before, but this time a hitch develops. An old life must sometimes be sacrificed not because it has become useless (as in "The Great Mountains"), but in order to make possible a new one. Nobody is at fault; the system is just not flawless. Jody has got what he wanted, but he has also learned what sacrifices men must sometimes make to achieve their ends.

The last story, "The Leader of the People," serves to climax the history of Jody's maturing. The story is linked skillfully with "The Promise" by Jody's first use in the cycle of the profanity he has picked up from Billy Buck at the end of the preceding story. When he says, "I hope it don't rain until after I kill them damn mice," he looks over his shoulder "to see whether Billy had noticed the mature profanity"; but Billy makes no comment.

This story is built around a visit from Jody's maternal grandfather, who had once led a group of migrants across the plains in pioneering days. Jody's father doesn't look forward to the visit because of the old man's ceaseless talk about his great experience. "He just goes on and on, and he never changes a word in the things he tells," the father complains; but Mrs.

Tiflin quietly replies, "That was the big thing in father's life. He led a wagon train across the plains to the coast, and when it was finished, his life was done. It was a big thing to do, but it didn't last long enough."

When the old man arrives, he begins talking again. Although Jody listens enthusiastically, there is tension in the air. The climax comes when Jody's father, thinking that the old man is out of earshot, asks with irritation, "Why does he tell [the stories] over and over? He came across the plains. All right! Now it's finished. Nobody wants to hear about it over and over." This time the old man overhears the complaint, and his spirit is broken. "Don't be sorry, Carl," he tells his son-in-law; "an old man doesn't see things sometimes. Maybe you're right. The crossing is finished. Maybe it should be forgotten, now it's done." Disconsolately, the old man sits on the porch. Jody remains loyal and learns in the course of their conversation the old man's real tragedy. He has not simply wished to reminisce about the old days to aggrandize himself. "I tell these old stories," he explains to Jody, "but they're not what I want to tell. I only know how I want people to feel when I tell them.... It wasn't getting here that mattered, it was movement and westering.... Then we came down to the sea, and it was done. That's what I should be telling instead of stories."

The tragedy is not just that the old man's work was ended too soon—that "there's a line of old men along the shore hating the ocean because it stopped them"—but that he is unable to communicate to the younger generation the feelings that motivated him. From this revelation Jody learns that just as nature is fallible, it—like man—has its limits, wears out, offers no new frontiers. Jody also learns something even more important—that the reason "nobody can tell you anything" is that experience may be incommunicable, impossible to share. The intent may be there, but the words are not adequate; therefore, he who would inspire the young seems just a long-winded old man.[7]

Jody also shows that he has learned even more. After listening to the old man, he offers to make him a lemonade. When his mother suggests that he wants to make one for the old man so that he can have one himself, he says, "No, Ma'am, I don't want one." She at first thinks him ill; then she recognizes that he wishes to make a truly altruistic gesture. Small as it is, it indicates that the boy has learned compassion—that he has entered into true adulthood (his knighthood), since he has learned that the only way to deal with the fallibility and the limitations of both men and nature is to be compassionate.

The morals are not so obvious in the stories as this explanation makes them seem, because Steinbeck succeeds in this cycle in so fusing his form and content that the complex "message" of the narrative is never forced, obtrusive, or verbose. In the depiction of a young man's emerging into compassionate adulthood by painfully learning through four crucial personal experiences of the fallibility of man, the wearing out of man, the unreliability of nature, and the exhaustion of nature, Steinbeck succeeds in doing what Jody's grandfather has failed to do—make his audience "feel" when he speaks. At the same time, the writer provides, through this fictional account of a boy who probably never heard of Emerson, a classic example of the transcendentalist's principle, expressed in "The American Scholar," of learning great truths of human experience through Nature and action rather than textbooks.

III *"Flight"*

The short story "Flight" is more difficult to date than *The Red Pony* because it first appeared in *The Long Valley* (1938), though Peter Lisca reports that several magazines rejected it in 1937. Perhaps it should not be discussed before *Tortilla Flat*, but in style and portentous tone it is closer to *To a God Unknown* than any other Steinbeck work. This story also provides an ideal bridge between *The Red Pony* and *Tortilla Flat* because its depressing account of an unprepared youth's failure to achieve maturity contrasts with Jody Tiflin's achievement and with the upbeat ending of *The Red Pony* and at the same time the story deals with the kind of Mexican-American characters that Steinbeck portrays with good-humored compassion in *Tortilla Flat*. Pepé's death in "Flight" at the hands of the mysterious and never identified "dark watchers" in the mountains also parallels the unaccountable death of Danny in *Tortilla Flat*.

The story also strikes the note of defeat that is sounded in Steinbeck's three novels preceding *The Grapes of Wrath*.

We could expect to find *The Red Pony* followed by the history of a grown-up Jody who uses his hard-bought wisdom to make the world a more comfortable place. But Steinbeck was not to be ready to extend his drama of consciousness beyond the threshold of manhood and to create this mature character until Tom Joad becomes Casy's disciple in *The Grapes of Wrath*. Indeed, Doc Burton, in *In Dubious Battle*, the only grown-up in this group of works who has Jody's insight, falls victim also to the "dark watchers."

Nineteen-year-old Pepé, the oldest child of a poor widow—unlike the clever, industrious Jody—is a lazy and not very bright boy who spends most of his time practicing flicking the knife that is his inheritance from his father. His mother feels at last, though, that she must entrust him with a mission to Monterey. Although he tells her, "You may send me often alone. I am a man," she is quite right in calling him "a foolish chicken." During a drunken quarrel in a friend's kitchen in town, he kills a man who calls him names that—as a man—he cannot allow. He is obliged to flee into the mountains, and there he becomes terrified when he sees "a dark form against the sky, a man's figure standing on top of a rock." After Pepé's horse is shot from under him, he struggles, desperately thirsty, up the rugged slope; but he still hears the faraway sounds of horses' hooves and a dog's yelping. Exhausted, he falls asleep and loses track of his rifle. A cut that a stone has made between his fingers results in the infection of the whole arm. He struggles to the peak of the ridge, but he has been followed. One bullet flies by him; then a second hits him in the chest. He topples from the rock, starting a little avalanche that "slid slowly down and covered up his head."

Despite its brevity, this story of a lonely flight to an inescapable death is reminiscent of Clyde Griffiths's in Theodore Dreiser's *An American Tragedy*. Pepé, like Clyde, is a cocky, impetuous, but mentally limited young man who is destroyed when a social situation places upon him responsibilities that he is unequipped to assume. This rare example of a Naturalistic story that satisfies even Edwin Cady's stringent definition is offered without a single editorial commentary—an achievement matched among Steinbeck's longer works only by *In Dubious Battle*.

IV   Tortilla Flat (1935)

"That is the way life goes, never the way you planned," philosophizes Pablo, a character in *Tortilla Flat*; but Pablo might well be the shade of Pepé, summarizing his bitter experience. Pablo illustrates his sweeping, downbeat generalization with the story of a dog-catcher named Tall Bob Smoke, who made a botch of everything he tried, even a suicide attempt that ended in his shooting off the end of his nose. We could scarcely find a better slogan for the kind of fiction that I have labeled Naturalistic or a better illustration than Tall Bob of those for whom life is indeed made up—as Stephen Crane put it—of "oaths and walking-sticks."

We may find it difficult to think of *Tortilla Flat* as a Naturalistic novel because of the stylized and somewhat condescending good humor with which Steinbeck approaches his characters. Writers like Frank Norris and Theodore Dreiser led us to expect Naturalistic fiction to be pontifical and humorless, for even these archattackers of the Genteel Tradition could not overcome its squeamish scruple that it is unseemly to be frivolous about human misery and degradation. Yet *Tortilla Flat* does share ultimately—despite its carnival atmosphere—the characteristic pessimism of most Naturalistic writing. However joyfully the *paisano* characters swagger toward their ends, the ends are not happy. For the like of this tale we must go back to Edgar Allen Poe's "The Masque of the Red Death" and "The Cask of Amontillado"—stories in which irresponsible festivities also have grisly conclusions.

Actually in this novel which first—deservedly—brought Steinbeck fame and fortune, the novelist succeeded in going further than any of his most outspoken predecessors in turning inside out the whole set of values and conventions associated with the Genteel Tradition, precisely as Poe had turned into horrors the aristocratic traditions of the South. Dreiser, Norris, Sinclair Lewis, even Hemingway before *The Old Man and the Sea*, had not in their denunciations of the arrogant rich been able to present an attractive alternative way of life that was not based upon access to wealth.

Steinbeck has a deserved reputation as a writer who rarely explains his work; but what actually occurs in *Tortilla Flat* has largely been obscured by a red herring dragged across the path by the author himself in a preface that compares Danny and his *paisano* friends to the knights of King Arthur's round table and in an often-quoted letter to his agents in which he offers to insert between chapters moral, esthetic, and historical interpretations "in the manner of the paisanos themselves."

Too much ingenuity has been expended—in the previous edition of this book, among other places—in pointing out Arthurian parallels. While I still think that there are more such parallels than some other commentators acknowledge, I refer those interested to my previous account; for I have come to believe that the important thing is that we recognize that, even if these parallels are present, they are not readily apparent to the reader and are not likely to affect his response to the story. We must also recall that Steinbeck did not provide the proffered interchapters—if he really seriously offered them—so that the novel must be judged on what it presents to the reader.

The point of *Tortilla Flat* is principally that the way of life of the "bums"—as respectable people might brand the *paisanos*—is superior to the average American's and that we might learn something from them; but the novel is also partially a warning that the simple life close to nature that some men long for is not the answer to the problems of either society or the individual. Steinbeck is here—as elsewhere—not so much exalting the have-nots as attacking the haves. As his viewpoint becomes increasingly sardonic and ironic during this Naturalistic period, Steinbeck is intimating that the unapologetic irresponsibility of the raffish *paisanos* has its shortcomings, but it is surely superior to the hypocritical high-mindedness of the equally unconsidered behavior of respectable Americans. *Tortilla Flat* is, in many ways, the Junius Maltby episode from *The Pastures of Heaven* blown up to book length and thrown in the faces of all the busybodying Munroes in the world.

The story of Danny is actually an extended illustration of Henry Morgan's observation in *Cup of Gold* that "civilization will split up a character, and he who refuses to split goes under." Danny is established in the preface as a kind of legendary wild man. Discharged from the army, he strolls along Alvarado Street breaking windows; jailed, he names dead bed-bugs for Monterey officials. He is an epic hero—the kind of unrestrained individual that many people oppressed by civilization would like to be and that the frustrated reader hopes can achieve a triumph over a stifling society that is vicariously the reader's own.

Tortilla Flat is not, however, a popular escapist fantasy; it is a fable that sugarcoats a bitter kernel. Danny does not flee soon enough into the forest; he confronts civilization too long and tries to make it come to terms with him instead of "splitting up" before it. His temptation comes in the form of two small houses that he inherits from his grandfather. Indeed, the outcome of the novel is foreshadowed even on the first page when we learn that, upon hearing about the houses, Danny "was a little weighted down with the responsibility of ownership." If this were escapist fiction, Danny would either dispose of the houses immediately or miraculously parlay them into a subdivision; instead, he moves into one and tries to live partly in the manner of a comfortable burgher, partly in a fashion superior to the burgher's by sharing his property with friends and aiding those in distress. His friend Pilon's observation, however, that "the worry of property was settling on Danny's face" is followed by the ominously significant remark that "No more in life would that face be free of care." Steinbeck implies that once man challenges civilization there is no drawing back.

For a while Danny and his company flourish by living in a "natural," uninhibited manner; they try—like Jesus Maria Corcoran—to relieve suffering and to look at girls' legs because they like to; or they express—like Big Joe—urges when they strike, even if the impulse is procreative and even if the place is the middle of a muddy street in view of a policeman. Nature, however, is not enough. As Danny settles down with his friends to a routine home life, he begins "to feel the beating of time," though he had never been conscious of clocks before. When he looks at his friends, he sees how "with them every day was the same," and he begins to long for the "good old days" when "the weight of property was not upon him." His friends try to help him, but "it was not coddling Danny wanted, it was freedom." In the end, he surrenders to his longing and disappears into the woods—only to find the wild life difficult and exhausting. Finally, he betrays his friends by selling his remaining house; when they repossess it by trickery, he is compelled to return, beaten and apathetic. To rouse him, his friends throw a party that becomes a legend.

At the height of the revelry Danny grows "huge and terrible" and, grabbing a table leg, challenges all present. When none will fight, he shouts, "Then I will go out to The One who can fight. I will find The Enemy who is worthy of Danny!" After he stalks out, his friends "heard his roaring challenge. . . . And then, behind the house, in the gulch, they heard an answering challenge so fearful and so chill that their spines wilted like nasturtium stems under frost. . . . They heard Danny charge to the fray. They heard his last shrill cry of defiance, and then a thump. And then silence."

Steinbeck never identifies the fearsome "Enemy." Each reader may interpret the term for himself as referring to God, fate, some cycle of nature, or whatever he envisions as imposing limits on man and as obliging him to conform to some system rather than live as a law unto himself. Maxwell Geismar argues perhaps most satisfactorily that this "enemy" is "the spectre of civilization within one's self."[8] Certainly Arthur Kinney's explanation that "Danny gets so drunk that he topples in stupor over a cliff to his death" is not adequate, for such an interpretation reduces the book to aimless slapstick.[9] Danny has set himself up against some kind of personal Moby Dick; and, like Ahab, he has been defeated. He refuses to "split up" before the demands of civilization; and—as Henry Morgan prophesied in *Cup of Gold*—he who will not split "goes under."

As a heroic tale, *Tortilla Flat* is a tragedy—as all of Steinbeck's previous writings had been from the point of view that whoever attempts to set himself above the crowd must compromise like Morgan or give up either his life or his dreams. Steinbeck does not editorialize about Danny's flaw—as he probably would have been tempted to do in a post–World War II novel; but he gives an inkling of it by having Danny observe of another man—a petty servant of civilization, that unfortunate dogcatcher, Tall Bob Smoke—that "It is not so easy to catch dogs when it is your business to catch dogs." It is easy to dream of freedom, but it is not easy to remain a free agent. Danny does not have the resources that enable him either to adjust to a new life or to revert to his old one; he cannot achieve the consciousness that would enable him to transcend his natural condition.

Interestingly, Danny's friend Pilon, who does know how to exercise conscious control over affairs, never gets an inheritance that might permit him to capitalize upon his abilities. It is difficult to believe that Pilon simply wanders off into the dark after Danny's death. Steinbeck, however, is not interested at this point in Pilon's fate. Nothing better illustrates the basically Naturalistic tenor of this richly comic invention than the author's focusing upon the doomed Danny, who is destroyed by his brush with civilization, rather than upon the traditionally picaresque figure of Pilon, who is capable of living by his wits.

Howard Levant has brilliantly argued that the conclusion of *Tortilla Flat* is flawed by Steinbeck's imposition of an arbitrarily predetermined order on the events—a tendency that Levant deems responsible for Steinbeck's future difficulties in plotting his stories.[10] I think that Levant's approach is quite sound if the novel is read—as it surely can be—as a conventional picaresque attack on respectable morality. In the last chapters, the episodic structure of the work is disrupted to move events rapidly toward a calamitous conclusion. But this conclusion is entirely fitting if the story is read not as a chronicle of roguery but—as Steinbeck hints it might be—as the tragical history of the defeat of Natural man. A change does occur in chapter 13 of the novel as the *paisano* band seems about to settle down to a conscious career of "do-gooding," when the men help Teresina Cortez feed her eight children. Pilon at the end of chapter 14 is devising a plan for getting free fish dinners; but, if the band settles down to this way of life, Pilon would have to become the leader and the novel would have to become his story.

Such intentions are neither Danny's nor Steinbeck's. This book is Danny's, and what begins to prey upon him especially is not even so much the ticking of the clock as the increasingly virtuous routine of the band's life as Pilon increasingly assumes leadership. While Danny's treacherous behavior near the end of the novel subverts his friends' desire for a comfortable place to rest their heads, their increasingly civilized ways have spurred this response in one who would like to remain a "natural man." Even the Pirate has begun to spend the quarters he earns for food that he brings home instead of hoarding them for the gloriously impractical purpose of buying a golden candlestick to repay St. Francis's graciousness to a mongrel dog. "The world is too much with us," William Wordsworth wrote just about the time that the *paisanos'* ancestors were arriving in the Monterey region. The world is surely too much with Danny, who does not find that civilization offers the individual enough to make compromise with it worthwhile.

Even the archaic chapter titles and language—the very Arthurian echoes—are not simply Steinbeck's attempts to be coy, whimsical, or condescending to a quaint ethnic group. The telling of the story in a style that sounds foreign to twentieth-century American ears serves to distance the reader from it—to make him feel that as much as he may admire some aspects of the carefree world of the *paisanos,* he can never actually enter it. *Tortilla Flat* is not one of the many tracts that circulated during the Depression advocating that urban Americans return to a simple pastoral life.[11] It is rather—as Steinbeck's preface suggests—a legend, presented in a manner that communicates the remoteness of the life of the *paisanos* from that of most of their compatriots. This legend is climaxed by a catastrophe that reminds us that we cannot escape responsibility for the complications of the worlds that we create. *Tortilla Flat* does not contradict Steinbeck's avowal in chapter 14 of *The Grapes of Wrath* that man must move forward, even if stumblingly and painfully; but it does clearly indicate that at the time he wrote the earlier novel Steinbeck could only envision these efforts as finally frustrated.

The Pastures of Heaven, The Red Pony, and *Tortilla Flat* are story-cycles not only in the formal sense that they incorporate anecdotes that can be separately read with pleasure into a loose framework that gives them additional meaning, but also in the philosophical sense that like other cyclical tales they show men returning after enormous exertions to create new worlds to a point like that from which they started. With the Whitesides' house burned in *The Pastures of Heaven,* Jody's grandfather's dream ended in "The Leader of the People," Danny's "round table" dispersed in *Tortilla Flat,* restless man in these works has been pitted against forces greater than he can master.

CHAPTER 5

Naturalism—Towards Theater

JUST after the New York opening of the much-acclaimed play version of *Of Mice and Men* on November 23, 1937, *Stage* magazine (January 1938) published a short article by Steinbeck in which he explained his intentions and argued that "the novel might benefit by the discipline and terseness of the stage." Actually, he had been moving towards theatrical style ever since he had abandoned the mannered styles of his earliest works. Both stage and screen producers had been quick to recognize the dramatic potential of *Tortilla Flat* (though both finally produced botched versions). Abandoning the cyclical form for a while after this novel, Steinbeck turned to stories that are tightly unified in their action and that are narrated almost entirely through dialogue. *Of Mice and Men*, of course, was intended for the stage; but even *In Dubious Battle* may be used for readers' theater with scarcely a change, and nearly all the stories in *The Long Valley* are tersely told and charged heavily with dramatic ironies.

I   In Dubious Battle *(1936)*

One thing that *The Red Pony* and *Tortilla Flat* are surely not is political. The "isms" of the modern world are remote from the California hills, and both stories are set just far enough in the past to provide an escape from the economic ills of the 1930s rather than the confrontation of them that Steinbeck presents in *The Grapes of Wrath*. As he moved toward dramatic presentation, however, he also moved towards this much more specific confrontation of bitter contemporary problems. *In Dubious Battle* has often been called the best novel about a strike ever written because Steinbeck refused to become a blind partisan and rather showed how struggles between laborers and employers—however provoked and justified—can inevitably prove only destructive and demoralizing to both parties and also to society as a whole. Neither Communists nor anti-Communists liked the novel because Steinbeck refused either to follow a strict Party line or to denounce the striking workers as un-American. The novel is not—like many others written during the same period—a narrowly legalistic attempt to indict one side or the other or a special pleading for sympathy that ignores the issues underlying labor disputes; rather it attacks dedication to any cause that leads people to exploit other human beings.

The leading characters of *In Dubious Battle* are, like those of *Tortilla Flat*, social outsiders that proper middle-class citizens would denounce as "riff-raff." What differentiates Mac and Jim in the strike novel from the *paisanos* of *Tortilla Flat* is their dedication to a "cause," an abstract theory about the conduct of society. They are motivated by their commitment to a specific, if limited, vision of life, so that they are ultimately not victims—as the hedonistic Danny is—of an unidentifiable force that looms between them and a perfect harmony with Nature. Instead they are victims of a particular program to which they commit themselves without taking the time or having the insight to grasp the implications of such commitment.

"We've got a job to do," Mack tells a character named Doc Burton in the novel. "We've got no time to mess around with high-falutin' ideas." "Yes," Burton replies, "and so you start your work not knowing your medium. And your ignorance trips you up every time" (147).[1] No exchange could better summarize the situation of the characters in what I am calling the *Naturalistic novel. In Dubious Battle* is Steinbeck's most pessimistic work, the only novel that might support some early critics' claims that the novelist's "biological" point of view equated men with other animals. In this book, not even the doctor, who analyzes and comments about situation that others fail to examine closely enough and who believes not in causes but "men," is able to save himself when violent passions are loosed. Although Burton claims that he does not wish to align himself with any cause that will place blinders on his vision, his position is as doctrinally *Naturalistic*—as I have been using the term—as the specifically political position of the Communist agitator-organizers. When Mac (one of the "reds") argues that "Revolution and communism will cure social injustice," Burton replies that "disinfection and prophylaxis will prevent" tetanus and syphilis. "It's different, though," Mac insists; "men are doing one, and germs are doing the other." "I can't see much difference, Mac," Burton replies glumly (144).

Although the novel portrays a violent strike in the Torgas Valley apple orchards of California, the narrative focuses upon the brief career as a Communist party activist of Jim Nolan, who doesn't want to be a "stooge" all his life. Jim wishes to join the party because he feels that his "whole family has been ruined" by the capitalist system. He has grown up in the "hopelessness" of certain defeat no matter how hard one struggles. His father had died as a result of labor violence; his mother has wasted away; and he has lost his job because of an unjustified charge of vagrancy when he is arrested while simply watching—not participating in—a radical demonstration. He feels dead because "everything in the past is gone" (9).

Sent to assist a veteran organizer (Mac) during the Torgas Valley operation, Jim discovers at last a meaning in life. "I'm happy for the first time. I'm full-up," he tells Doc Burton after he is shot in the shoulder during the strike violence. He begins to develop a sense of leadership, and he tells his partner, "I'm stronger than you, Mac. I'm stronger than anything in the world, because I'm going in a straight line. You and all the rest have to think of women and tobacco and liquor and keeping warm and fed.... I wanted to be used. Now I'll use you, Mac. I'll use myself and you. I tell you, I feel there's strength in me" (274).

London, the leader of the striking workers, is amazed to discover that "One minute [Jim's] a blabber-mouth kid, and the next minute, by Christ, he just boots me out and takes over" (282). But Jim's moment of glory is short-lived. Tricked by vigilantes seeking to break the strike, Jim and Mac rush into an ambush. Mac is experienced enough to save himself; but Jim, whose enthusiasm has outrun his know-how, has his face blown off by a shotgun. Mac drags the faceless body back to rally the strikers, whose spirits have been sagging. Letting a lantern's light fall on the mutilated boy, Mac begins, "This guy didn't want nothing for himself——Comrades! He didn't want nothing for himself——" (343). Jim has not only been used in life and in death; he has been wasted. As Doc Burton had protested, "It all seems meaningless to me, brutal and meaningless.... You can only build a violent thing with violence" (252–53).

Even had Jim survived the strike, his commitment to the

"cause," Steinbeck intimates, would have dehumanized him, just as Mac has been dehumanized by it. Mac can think only in terms of using people to produce the results he wants. When Burton observes that Mac can imitate the speech of any group that he is talking with, Mac explains, "men are suspicious of a man who doesn't talk their way. You can insult a man pretty badly by using a word he doesn't understand" (142). That his thoughts are of the Cause rather than of other's feelings becomes evident when he explains to Jim that "we can't waste time liking people" (115) and that "I can't take time to think about the feelings of one man . . . I'm too busy with big bunches of men" (201). Mac admits that the strike may not succeed, but he justifies it on the ground that "The thing will carry on and on. It'll spread, and some day—it'll work. Some day we'll win" (155). "You're a cold-blooded bastard. Don't you think of nothing but 'strike'?" one of the laborers' leaders grimaces when Mac explains that they must use one man's death "to step our guys up, to keep 'em together. This'll stick 'em together, this'll make 'em fight" (164). When Mac brutally beats a high school boy who has been urged to attack the strikers by a bullying crowd, another strike leader observes with horror, "Jesus, you're a cruel bastard, Mac. I can unda'stand a guy gettin' mad an' doin' it, but you wasn't mad." "I know," Mac replies. "That's the hardest part," as he smiles coldly (273).

Yet Mac is finally not equal to the burden he has taken upon himself. When a sympathizer's lunch wagon is burned by vigilantes, Mac says, "Jesus! I didn't think they'd do that." He has not an adequate organization to prevent a sympathetic farmer's barn filled with apples from being burned. He has a tactical ability to manipulate men, but he lacks the long view of the strategist. "How you goin' to get guys to fight when they want to run?" a strike leader asks. "I don't know," Mac is obliged to reply. "We can try to make 'em fight by talkin' to 'em." When Doc Burton tries to theorize about the leader's relationship to group man, Mac says with disgust, "This isn't practical." "I don't know why I go on talking, then," Burton says, laughing. "You practical men always lead practical men with stomachs. And something always gets out of hand. Your men get out of hand, they don't follow the rules of common sense, and you practical men either deny that it is so, or refuse to think about it. And when someone wonders what it is that makes a man with a stomach something more than your rule allows, why you howl, 'Dreamer, mystic, metaphysician!! . . .' In all history there are no men who have come to such wild-eyed confusion and bewilderment as practical men leading men with stomachs" (147).

Burton assists the strikers because he feels he must help, but he refuses to become committed to any cause. He seems to offer an alternative to the organizers who lack the vision to control the forces that they conjure up. When Mac asks the doctor whether he doesn't think that the cause is good, Burton replies: "My senses aren't above reproach, but they're all I have. I want to see the whole picture—as nearly as I can. I don't want to put on the blinders of 'good' and 'bad,' and limit my vision. If I used the term 'good' on a thing I'd lose my license to inspect it because there might be some bad in it. Don't you see? I want to be able to look at the whole thing" (143).

Burton is striving for as complete self-consciousness as possible; but, in this most pessimistic of Steinbeck's novels, the consciously thoughtful man is as doomed as those who are incapable of examining their commitments. While Jim feels that the violence epitomized by the strike can only stop "when the men rule themselves and get the profit of their labors," Burton can only observe, "seems simple enough . . . I wish I thought it was so simple" (252). But, when Burton acknowledges that Jim sees a way through the struggle, he can only add, "I wish I did." His introspection has not provided the answers that another Doc finds at the end of *Cannery Row.* Indeed, Burton of *In Dubious Battle* is not even allowed to survive to see the fulfillment of his predictions about the collapse of the too hastily improvised strike; for, on his way one night to visit a wounded man, he simply disappears. So far as we know, he doesn't even come to a violent end; he simply disappears. There is no survival for the man of goodwill and thoughtful speculation in the Naturalistic world in which "ignorant armies clash by night."

The "battle" of the novel's title is "dubious"—not because there is doubt about which side will win but because there are doubts about the merits of both sides. Steinbeck speaks much later in *A Russian Journal* of the "ecclesiastical left" and the "lumpen right," and he doubts his ability to satisfy either. *In Dubious Battle* shows these two parties in action. Steinbeck's novel is not—like much other American writing from the 1930s—either an all-out attack on the capitalist system or a denunication of the Reds. It is rather an attack on any fiercely held partisan abstraction that denies and destroys the dignity of the individual human being.

II   The Long Valley *(1938)*

Most closely related to *In Dubious Battle* and illustrative of the same despairing philosophy are two stories collected in *The Long Valley*, "The Raid" and "The Vigilante." Peter Lisca argues that "The Raid," first published in 1934, may have been conceived as an episode for the novel or as part of a biographical sketch that Steinbeck was writing about an actual labor organizer.[2] Actually, the story is scarcely more than an excruciatingly suspenseful account—which could be transferred to the stage almost without change—of two labor organizers who are waiting for an angry mob to descend upon them. It does, however, lay heavy stress on a point that is made less central to the argument of *In Dubious Battle*.

Several times in this novel Doc Burton suggests that Jim shows an almost religious enthusiasm for his cause; when Jim angrily rejects the suggestion that religion has anything to do with it because it is only a group of men, Burton asks, "Well, can't a group of men be God, Jim?" But Jim, who refuses to pursue the discussion, charges Burton with building "a trap of words" (255). Dick and Root in "The Raid," however, are sensitive to the "religious" aspects of their work and seem deliberately to cultivate martyrdom. When Root expresses his fear of being beaten by the mob, the older Dick tells him, "I don't know much, but I been through this mill before. I can tell you this for sure. When it comes—it won't hurt. I don't know why, but it won't. Even if they kill you it won't hurt." After they are beaten, Root confirms Dick's remarks, "It didn't hurt, Dick. It was funny. I felt all full up—and good." Dick becomes uncomfortable, however, when Root presses further, "You remember in the Bible, Dick, how it says, something like, 'Forgive them because they don't know what they're doing'?" Dick advises the other to "lay off that religion stuff" because "religion is the opium of the people." The teachings of a religion may persist, however, even beyond the death of its particular forms. The sentiments that Casy articulates in *The Grapes of Wrath* are stirring in the minds of earlier Steinbeck characters—even those that he manipulates to create his darkest Naturalistic ironies.

"The Vigilante," a brief vignette of a man on his way home after participating in a lynching, might well be printed as an appendix to *In Dubious Battle* because it provides insight into Steinbeck's conception of a matter not treated in the novel—the inner feelings of the self-righteous persecutors of the strikers. The touch of artistic vision that makes this extremely impersonal episode more than something that might have been copied from the newspapers of the day is manifested after the man arrives home from the lynching:

His thin, petulant wife was sitting by the open gas oven warming herself. She turned complaining eyes on Mike where he stood in the doorway.

Then her eyes widened and hung on his face. "You been with a woman," she said hoarsely. . . .

He walked through the kitchen and went into the bathroom. A little mirror hung on the wall. Mike took off his cap and looked at his face. "By God, she was right," he thought, "That's just exactly how I do feel."

Participating in the lynching has provided him with something missing in his relationship with the "thin, petulant wife." Energy that should be expended in love has been diverted into violence. Mike's final interview with his wife—nearly as horrifying as the lynching itself—links this story with the largest group collected in *The Long Valley*—stories that in one way or another present the consequences of a situation stressed by Jim Moore's realization in "The Murder" that "he could not get in touch with [his wife] in any way."

Women play remarkably small roles in the fiction of Steinbeck's Naturalistic period. Peripheral figures in *Tortilla Flat*, they are viewed by Danny's friends either as easy targets for propositions or as threats to the men's comradeship. The only female character of any importance in *In Dubious Battle* appears only to provide Mac with a chance to ingratiate himself with the fruit-pickers he wants to organize by delivering one of the leaders' grandson. In the short stories, however, the women are often the forces that bring the underlying problems to a head.

Only one of the stories, the frequently anthologized "The Chrysanthemums," treats a frustrated woman sympathetically by portraying her as the victim of an unscrupulous confidence man; and this tale has had a curious history. For years no one noticed that there were two versions circulating: the texts in *Harper's* magazine (October, 1937) and in *The Long Valley* differ. The differences are not extensive enough to alter the basic relationships in the story, although the *Harper's* version tones down the sexual implications.[3] In both versions, Elisa, a strong, childless woman of thirty-five, has sublimated her maternal instincts by producing remarkable flowers. When an itinerant tinker wanders by her ranch, he inveigles her into giving him some work to do by praising her plants. She even prepares some chrysanthemum cuttings for him to take to a woman down the road; but on the way to town that night with her husband Elisa spots the treasured slips lying along the road, although the tinker has kept the pot. A principal difference between the two versions occurs in the description of her reaction:

In a moment they had left behind them the man who had not known or needed to know what she said, the bargainer. She did not look back. (*Harper's*).

. . .

In a moment it was over. The thing was done. She did not look back. (*The Long Valley*)

Through examination of the manuscripts at the Humanities Research Center of the University of Texas at Austin, Roy S. Simmonds has established that the passage in *The Long Valley* version of the story substantially existed in the manuscript from the beginning. Simmonds infers that modifications in the original story were made by or for the editor of the "genteel" magazine and that the original passages were restored when Steinbeck prepared the manuscript for the book.[4] The changes for the magazine story, however, simply left less to the reader's imagination. (Elisa's remark in the book version, for example, that "every pointed star gets driven into your body" does not appear in *Harper's*.) In both versions, Elisa and the tinker are unique among Steinbeck's creations. In most of his other stories women are the temptresses, and the well-intentioned men suffer from their machinations.

The simplest of these tales, "The Snake," describes a woman who visits a marine biological laboratory and buys a male rattlesnake, which she then insists be fed a laboratory rat. The biologist sickens as the woman begins to sway, "not much, just a suggestion," as the snake begins to weave before striking the rat. After the snake has killed the rat and prepared to swallow it, "Dr. Phillips put his will against his head to keep from turning toward the woman. He thought, 'If she's opening her mouth, I'll be sick. I'll be afraid.' " He vows that if she returns, he will go out and leave her alone; but she never comes back.

Loneliness is the common characteristic of the men in the other stories. Peter Randall in "The Harness" is "one of the most highly respected farmers in Monterey County," but after his sickly, eighty-seven pound wife finally dies, the control that she exercised over him is revealed when he confesses to a friend that she forced him to wear a web harness as a physical symbol of his psychological enslavement and that he had been able to resist her only enough to make one annual "business trip" of a week's duration, during which he actually got drunk in San Francisco and visited "fancy houses." His wife dead, he refuses to eat any more of the cakes that well-meaning people used to send when the wife had her annual illness after his return from the "business trip"; and he also takes off the oppressive harness. He even plants his whole fifty-five acres in a fragrant, but recklessly speculative crop of sweet peas—something that his wife would never have permitted. His gamble pays when the weather proves just right for the crop, but he is still not happy. Speaking of his wife to the friend, he confides, "She didn't die dead. . . . She won't let me do things. She's worried me all year about those peas." He refuses to wear the harness again, but he resumes his annual trips to San Francisco.

Two other men strike back at their female oppressors. Mary Teller in "The White Quail" is the most unattractive woman in Steinbeck's fiction before the incredible Kate Trask of *East of Eden.* Mary's whole life is centered upon creating a perfect garden; indeed, the question she asks even in choosing a husband is not, "Would this man like such a garden, but would the garden like such a man?" Harry Teller, who runs a loan agency, is the perfect stooge: he not only humors her plans for the garden but gives up his own hopes of having a dog because it might ruin the plants. He also suffers himself to be locked out of her bedroom and to endure an attack on his business ethics because she feels—with an irony almost too heavy-handed in view of her own condition—that "a little mental housecleaning mightn't be a bad thing for Harry." When Mary begins to identify with a remarkable albino quail that visits the garden, she suffers the first setback to her total domination of Harry after he refuses to poison a cat that threatens the bird. When he agrees to scare the cat away with an air gun, he kills the white quail, though he claims he didn't mean to do so. "What a dirty skunk, to kill a thing she loved so much," he cries; but he drops his head and adds, "I'm lonely. . . . Oh, Lord, I'm so lonely."

Mary is pathological. Early in the story she looks at "the dark thickets of the hill" beyond her garden and says "That's the enemy. . . . That's the world that wants to get in, all rough and tangled and unkempt. But it can't get in because the fuchsias won't let it. That's what the fuchsias are for. . . ." Harry is a victim of his own lack of enough fortitude to do something about the situation, possibly because of some unacknowledged guilt feelings about his exploitative business. But Steinbeck is principally concerned with trying to create and condemn a person who has become so obsessed with realizing a dream as to become isolated from all normal human relationships.

The husband in "The Murder" finally consciously takes matters into his own hands. When he marries a Jugo-Slav girl, her father tells him, "Don't be big fool, now. . . . Jelka is Slav girl. He's not like American girl. If he is bad; beat him. If he's good too long, beat him too. I beat his mamma. Papa beat my mama. Slav girl! He's not like a man that don't beat hell out of him." Properly American Jim Moore says only, "I wouldn't beat Jelka." He discovers that she is "a fine wife, but there was no companionship in her." He cannot get in touch with her, though her remoteness is "neither hostile nor intentional." Coming home earlier than he planned one night,

Jim finds his wife in bed with her cousin; he kills the cousin and does at last thrash Jelka. "You hurt me bad," she says. "Bad as I could without killing you," he replies. She begins making his breakfast, as he lays plans for a new house. "Will you whip me any more—for this?" she asks. "No, not any more, for this," he replies. She smiles as he strokes her hair.

Since there appears to be nothing subnormal about Jelka, it is difficult today to read "The Murder" as anything except evidence that Steinbeck conceived of "Jugo-Slav girls" as almost parodies of what I have been calling Naturalistic characters. It is perhaps a mark of the tastes of the times that in the 1930s this was his first story to be selected for the annual O. Henry prize collection, which failed to include "The Gift" or "The Great Mountains." The manifest racial and antifeminist prejudices make the story objectionable today, but, when read in the context of *The Long Valley*, it can be seen as simply another of Steinbeck's mordantly ironic commentaries on the lack of sympathetic communication between human beings that seems to make inescapable the violence that Doc Burton deplores in *In Dubious Battle*.

Hints of ethnic prejudice appear in the most pathetic and bitterly ironic tale in the collection, "Johnny Bear," the only one besides "The Chrysanthemums" to portray a woman as a victim, not of a "bargainer," but of social and familial prejudices.[5] "Johnny Bear" is also the story most closely related to *Of Mice and Men*; for the title character, like Lennie in the play-novelette, is subnormal. A native of the village of Loma tells a visitor about him: " . . . Blind Tom was a half-wit. He could hardly talk, but he could imitate anything he heard on the piano. . . . Johnny Bear is the same. Only he can photograph words and voices. [A man] tested Johnny with a long passage in Greek and Johnny did it exactly. He doesn't know the words he's saying, he just says them. He hasn't brains enough to make anything up, so you know that what he says is what he heard."

The story is not concerned, however, with Johnny's fate; he is simply the only vehicle through which the secret history that is the real matter of the story becomes public. The same man who has told the story of Johnny tells the outsider, "Every town has its aristocrats, its family above reproach. Emalin and Amy Hawkins are our aristocrats. . . . They're symbols. They're what we tell our kids when we want to—well, to describe good people."

But the Hawkins sisters are not exempt from the eavesdropping of Johnny Bear, who, in return for whiskeys at the local bar, reveals that the weaker of the two sisters has become pregnant and has hanged herself. But even the hanging does not climax the story; for Johnny's most staggering revelation is that she has been sleeping with a Chinaman, a member—in small-town California—of a despised race. This woman, who in the eyes of the community has lived "as though honesty really is the best policy and charity really is its own reward," has suffered such loneliness that she has been driven to a proscribed course that can end only in suicide.

Nowhere in these nine stories written in the middle of the 1930s are the characters able to control or even to understand their behavior. Together they comprise, with the two episodic novels that might be called groups of short stories (*The Pastures of Heaven* and *Tortilla Flat*) and with the two short novels that are really only extended episodes moving like short stories towards a single climax (*In Dubious Battle* and *Of Mice and Men*), one of the most remarkable and consistent bodies of Naturalistic writing in American literature. Steinbeck's much-discussed nonteleological concern with "how" things happened rather than with "why" (he confessed in "About Ed Ricketts" that "The Snake" recorded an actual incident, but that he didn't know what it meant)[6] may have caused him to choose material that dramatized the philosophy—or the material may have influenced the development of the philosophy. Whatever the cause-and-effect relationship, a close connection certainly exists between the Naturalistic and nonteleological points of view.

III Of Mice and Men (1937)

Steinbeck's preoccupation with Ed Ricketts's nonteleological concepts that *what* things are matters less than the fact that they *are*[7] led to the Naturalistic fable that precipitated the novelist into national celebrity, *Of Mice and Men*, which had once simply been titled "Something that Happened." This narrative differs from Steinbeck's earlier ones in that it was deliberately conceived as a novelette that might be turned without revision into a play. This unconventional idea was warmly greeted by a Broadway theater that was desperately searching for gimmicks that might help revive what was then known as "the fabulous invalid" laid low by the Depression and the competition from talking pictures. In fact, *Of Mice and Men* was staged the same season that Thornton Wilder's *Our Town* created a sensation by being played without scenery. When the short book became a Book-of-the-Month Club selection and a best seller, famed playwright and play-doctor George S. Kaufman helped Steinbeck prepare the acting version. Rights were sold to Hollywood; and, despite the censorship problems that the story posed in Hays Office days, it was finally—in the wake of the success of *The Grapes of Wrath*—turned into a powerful film.

Again, as in many of the short stories, a woman precipitates the tragic denouement; but this girl is herself—like Amy Hawkins in "Johnny Bear"—as much a victim as her victims. The real villain is her violent and insensitive husband; but he, too, cannot really be held responsible for the deaths at the end because he is scarcely more intelligent than the hulking innocent who becomes his prey. The whole affair is simply "something that happened"—all the characters find their world to be made of "oaths and walking-sticks," and their dreams are the only things that can keep them going. This view was likely to be particularly popular in the middle of the 1930s when many people regarded themselves as helpless victims of forces beyond their control. Many readers surely found easier identification with this story than with Steinbeck's earlier works since he wrote here not about an exotic ethnic group, as in *Tortilla Flat*, or about widely disliked "red" agitators, as in *In Dubious Battle*, but about rural American boys who, down on their luck, still dreamed the American dream of owning a little place of their own. "Nobody never gets to heaven; and nobody gets no land," Crooks, the Negro stable buck, observes cynically when he hears of George and Lennie's dream of owning a farm; and he summarizes the vision behind the work.

The action begins with George and Lennie, two itinerant ranch hands, who are preparing to start a new job. What differentiates this pair from the ordinary stumblebums then circulating the country in droves is the dream they share that George chants to Lennie's delight as they rest in a grove of willows: "Guys like us, that work on ranches, are the loneliest guys in the world. They got no family. They don't belong no place.... With us it ain't like that. We got a future...." At this point Lennie breaks in to help finish the familiar chant: *"because I got you to look after me, and you got me to look after you, and that's why."* In the bunkhouse of their new employers, Slim, "a jerkline skinner, the prince of the ranch," observes that there "ain't many guys travel around together.... Maybe ever'body in the whole damn world is scared of each other."

George and Lennie have joined forces because, although George maintains that Lennie "ain't no cuckoo," he is undeniably overdeveloped physically and underdeveloped mentally—a powerful gaint with an infant's brain. George has promised Lennie's aunt to look out for the giant; but, although George often complains of the demands that the commitment makes upon him, he derives from it the benefit of having someone to take care of and to share his dream of independence on a small ranch. This dream is sufficiently persuasive to win Candy, a handicapped bunkhouse swamper, whose old dog is killed by an unsentimental ranch hand who lives only by his sensations. The dream also tempts the cynical Negro Crooks out of the misanthropy resulting from his ostracism by the white hands.

The hopelessness of the dream is suggested, however, in the opening chapter when George and Lennie's conversation reveals that they have had to run away from their last job because of Lennie's supposedly molesting a girl. Lennie is also treasuring a dead mouse, for he loves to pet soft things. Because of his great strength and his lack of mental control, he unavoidably kills these things he loves; and, though George strives desperately to keep Lennie out of trouble, the dim-witted giant keeps finding mice, puppies, and girls to maul.

George senses trouble at the new location as soon as he meets Curley, the ranch-owner's son; a cocky lightweight fighter, he—as Candy explains—"hates big guys.... Kind of like he's mad at 'em because he ain't a big guy." Curley has recently married a girl whom Candy calls a "tart," and he is having trouble keeping track of her. Despite George's efforts, Curley picks a fight with Lennie and bloodies the giant's nose. Exasperated, George orders the reluctant Lennie to fight back, and Curley's hand is crushed. George and Lennie are afraid of losing their jobs, but Slim, the foreman, warns Curley that he will look ridiculous if his defeat is known.

Curley is silenced, but his wife is less easy to control. A restless, overpainted girl, her dreams of going to Hollywood have been encouraged by a casual date who took her to the cheap dancehall where she met Curley. Her intrusion into a Saturday night conversation between Lennie, Candy, and Crooks, after the hands have gone to town, is resented. Even though rejected by these "weak ones," she persists in forcing her attentions on Lennie on Sunday afternoon while the others are preoccupied by a horseshoe tournament. She gets Lennie to feel her soft hair; but, when he begins to muss it, she panics; and he breaks her neck.

We cannot sympathize with the girl. On Saturday night when Crooks tries to get her to leave the barn, she threatens him: "Well, you keep your place then, Nigger. I could get you strung up on a tree so easy it ain't even funny." Yet when she is dead, Steinbeck observes in one of the few departures from his dramatic objectivity in the narration: "Curley's wife lay with a half-covering of yellow hay. And the meanness and the plannings and the discontent and the ache for attention were all gone from her face. She was very pretty and simple, and her face was sweet and young. Now her rouged cheeks and her reddened lips made her seem alive and sleeping very lightly."

When George discovers what has happened, he realizes that his dream is ended. He pursues Lennie to a grove where they had agreed to meet should trouble develop. There, in a nightmarish sequence, George shoots Lennie before the other men, led by Curley—bent on lynching—can reach him. Although George's hand shakes violently, he sets his face and pulls the trigger; and, by doing so, he not only saves Lennie from the painful, but to him incomprehensible, vengeance of his pursuers, but also completely destroys the dream that has given George's own life a direction and meaning.

Slim, who comprehends the situation, consoles George by telling him that he had to do what he did; but the last word is assigned to the unfeeling dog-killer, who can only say with puzzlement, "Now what the hell ya suppose is eatin' them two guys." "The best laid schemes o' mice an' men/ Gang aft a-gley" (in Robert Burns's familiar words) because even the man who has achieved a certain amount of control over his instincts and his fellowman—like George—is helpless in the hands of an indifferent, imperfect nature. Although the play follows the narrative of the novel, it misses this final point and stresses the sensational aspects of the plot by ending with the killing.

Slim's final attempt to console George ends the novel on the same compassionate note as that of *The Red Pony*, but Slim can only alleviate, not cure, the situation. A grown-up Jody Tiflin, he brings what comfort he can to one who has been obliged not just to witness the death of his dream but to strike the fatal blow himself. But *Of Mice and Men* is Steinbeck's last work for a long time to end on such a note of resignation. His next heroes—who truly merit that appellation—will make, even in going down to defeat, bold gestures that indicate that they intend to improve conditions or to die trying rather than "splitting up" before implacable forces or dying without recognizing the opponents they challenge.

CHAPTER 6

From Naturalism to the Drama of Consciousness—The Education of the Heart in The Grapes of Wrath

A PPARENTLY the novel that was to become *The Grapes of Wrath* (1939) was written originally in the same bitterly ironic, pessimistic vein as *In Dubious Battle* and *Of Mice and Men.* In a letter to his agents and publishers in June, 1938, Steinbeck announced the decision that marked the most significant turning point in his career as an artist. He called a sixty-five thousand word novel, which was tentatively entitled "L'Affaire Lettuceberg," a "bad book"—what his father would have called "a smart-alec book"—and announced that it could not be published. "My whole work drive has been aimed at making people understand each other," he continued; "and then I deliberately write this book, the aim of which is to cause hatred through partial understanding."[1]

Steinbeck pushed himself to finish a new version by autumn; and the result was *The Grapes of Wrath*, a novel that begins—with its description of a land devastated by dust storms and the slow, determined plodding of a land turtle—like the Naturalistic works that Steinbeck had been writing for nearly a decade. However, the narrative becomes something quite different—a story of the awakening of man's consciousness that coincides with the awakening of his conscience. This change is signaled in the fourteenth chapter by an interpolated credo about the uniqueness of man: "This you may say of man—when theories change and crash, when schools, philosophies, when narrow dark alleys of thought, national, religious, economic, grow and disintegrate, man reaches, stumbles forward, painfully, mistakenly sometimes. Having stepped forward, he may slip back, but only half a step, never the full step back" (204–05).[2] This credo underlies Steinbeck's fiction for the rest of his life, and it is given its final form in his pronouncement during his Nobel Prize acceptance speech: "I hold that a writer who does not passionately believe in the perfectibility of man has no dedication nor any membership in literature."

The writer of *In Dubious Battle* and *Of Mice and Men* gives no evidence of believing in the perfectibility of man; the writer who rewrote "L'Affaire Lettuceberg" into *The Grapes of Wrath* does. The central story of the big novel is of the Joad family's taking the step forward that Steinbeck describes in the fourteenth chapter. This novel is not a *static* one about long-suffering Jobs; it is a *dynamic* one about people who learn that survival depends upon their adapting to new conditions. This point—that the novel tells a dynamic story about learning to change—has often, however, been missed, as is illustrated by widespread misconceptions about the tableau that unmistakably ends the story that Steinbeck has chosen to tell, even though it presents no lasting solution to the real-life situation of the migrant workers who inspired the fiction.

In the final chapter, Ma Joad leads the remnants of her "fambly" from their flood-engulfed boxcar to a dry barn on high land. There Rosasharn, whose baby has been stillborn, feeds from her breast an old man on the point of death who cannot be nourished otherwise. Although it would seem that only the prurient, who have missed the point that the plight of these people is desperate, could object to this poignant scene, it has been a bone of contention since the novel appeared. Among the early reviewers, Clifton Fadiman wrote in the *New Yorker*, that "the ending is the tawdriest kind of fake symbolism." Later, French critic Claude-Edmond Magny argued that the novel ends on "a purely poetic image which in no way brings the plot to a conclusion." Even such a standard reference work as James Hart's *Oxford Companion to American Literature* maintains the position that Steinbeck fails to complete his story, "the value of whose conclusion is purely symbolic." Thus it is charged either that the conclusion concludes nothing or that it is not prepared for by any overall allegorical structure. My thesis is that both charges are wrong and that the Joad story in *The Grapes of Wrath* is—like *The Red Pony*—a consistent allegory that is concluded logically and fittingly by Rosasharn's gesture and that, furthermore—as the author himself suggests—a reader may find "five layers" in the book.[3]

In a sociological sense, of course, the novel is unfinished because Steinbeck does not tell us whether the migrants survive or disappear. At the time he wrote, he didn't know what the outcome of their struggles would be. He implied, however, that the actions of the reader might have a bearing on the situation, just as a great predecessor had in a novel that is in many ways similar and that certainly might have lent its title to Steinbeck's. At the end of *Hard Times*, Charles Dickens directly addresses his "Dear reader": "it rests with you and me, whether, in our two fields of action, similar things shall be or not. Let them be!" As for the solution of the real problems that the novels reflect, Dickens and Steinbeck leave it to the readers in their "field of action"—the real world; the novelist's field of action is literary allegory, not sociological prophecy.

I   *The Education of the Heart*

The story of the Joads, insofar as it concerns the novelist, is completed in the barn; for the novel is not about the family's quest for security but about their education, which is shown to be completed in the final scene.

What "education"?—the education of the heart, the same kind of education that Thomas Gradgrind receives painfully in *Hard Times* and that provides the principal link between these two powerful and controversial works. In *The Grapes of Wrath*, this education results in a change from the family's jealously regarding itself as an isolated and self-important clan to its envisioning itself as part of one vast human family that, in preacher Casy's words, shares "one big soul ever'body's a part of" (33). The novel is not so much concerned with the frustrating physical migration described—much as Steinbeck's unsparing picture of contemporary conditions may have accounted for the phenomenal reception of the novel—as with the accompanying spiritual movement that is akin to the one celebrated in Walt Whitman's "Passage to India."

Casy, the former preacher, has already meditated upon the idea of a brotherhood of all men before the story begins, but he cannot formulate clearly his concept. He finds it difficult to explain his idea that "maybe it's all men an' all women we love" (32) because "fella gets use' to a way of thinkin', it's hard to leave" (69). When he finds confirmation of his theory in Muley Graves's observation, "If a fella's got somepin to eat an' another fella's hungry—why, the first fella ain' got no choice," Casy feels obliged to say, "Muley's got a-holt of somepin, an' it's too big for him, an' it's too big for me" (66). The difficulty of clarifying his new idea had become evident when he and Tom Joad had reached the deserted Joad house and Casy had confessed, "If I was still a preacher I'd say the arm of the Lord has struck. But now I don't know what's happened" (55). Still, he is able to exemplify his new ideas when he replies to Ma Joad's objection that cutting pork is women's work, "It's all work. . . . They's too much of it to split up to men's or women's work" (146).

When Casy finally figures out in a California jail what he does believe, he explains his ideas in the form of a parable that illustrates the benefits of unified action. Speaking of the inmates, he says,

"Well, they was nice fellas, ya see. What made 'em bad was they needed stuff. An' I begin to see, then. It's need that makes all the trouble. I ain't got it worked out. Well, one day they give us some beans that was sour. One fella started yellin', an' nothin' happened. He yelled his head off. Trusty come along an' looked in an' went on. Then another fella yelled. Well, sir, then we all got yellin'. And we all got on the same tone. . . . Then somepin happened! They come a-runnin', and they give us some other stuff to eat—give it to us. Ya see? (521–22).

At the moment, Tom Joad doesn't see; and Casy observes, "Maybe I can't tell you. . . . Maybe you got to find out" (522). The novel depicts the Joads' "finding out."

They are a difficult case, for *The Grapes of Wrath* is not a tale of the conversion of the easily susceptible. The family's haughty, isolated attitude at the beginning of the novel is illustrated by Tom's remark to a friendly truckdriver: "Nothin' ain't none of your affair except skinnin' this here bull-bitch along, an' that's the least thing you work at" (18). Tom is not a thinker. When Casy tells him, "They's gonna come a thing that's gonna change the whole country," Tom simply replies, "I'm still layin' my dogs down one at a time" (237). Uncle John, who has been responsible for his wife's death, comes closest to understanding that something exists that is beyond the family, but he attributes the failures that result from his selfishness to "sin," and he indulges in disorganized acts of charity that lead Pa Joad to comment that he "give away about ever'thing he got, an' still he ain't very happy" (92).

Ma, whom Steinbeck calls "the citadel of the family" (100), views the trip to California only in terms of the family's success. She ponders, "I wonder—that is, if we all get jobs an' all work—maybe we can get one of them little white houses" (124). Although she burns her souvenirs to sever herself from her past (148), she does so because she thinks primarily of her importance to the family. When Tom asks if she's not "scared" that the new place won't be "nice like we thought," she replies, "No, I ain't. . . . Up ahead they's a thousan' lives we might live, but when it comes, it'll on'y be one. . . . it's jus' the road goin' by for me. . . . All the rest'd get upset if I done any more'n that. They all depen' on me jus' thinkin' about that" (168–69).

When Ma threatens Pa with a jack-handle to prevent the family's splitting up, she argues, "All we got is the family unbroke. Like a bunch of cows, when the lobos are ranging, stick all together. I ain't scared while we're all here, all that's alive, but I ain't gonna see us bust up" (231). She still seeks rationalizations that will incorporate the Wilsons into the family rather than make assistance to them appear to be help to strangers. "We got almost a kin bond," she tells Sairy; "Grampa, he died in your tent" (227). And she insists that Casy not write the note to be pinned to Grampa's body because the preacher "wan't no kin" (195).

But the family disintegrates in spite of Ma's brave efforts and her bold protests. The dog is killed on the highway. Grampa dies of a stroke before the family crosses the Oklahoma border, and Granma dies before they have reached the fertile valleys of California. Because each death symbolizes an inability to adjust to the changed conditions imposed by the migration, it does not challenge the family's basic unity. Ma is more severely shaken by the departure of the oldest son Noah to live "beside a nice river" (284), and she is forced to observe, "Family's fallin' apart. . . . I don' know. Seems like I can't think no more" (294). Most alarming, however, is the disappearance of Rose of Sharon's husband Connie Rivers because his running away shatters a potential family unit that is just in the process of forming.

Ma's family pride is shattered in other ways. She is disturbed by the California border patrolman from whom she first hears the term "Okie" when he tells her, "We don't want none of you settlin' down here" (291). Then she is upset by the vigilance committee which warns the family, "We ain't gonna have no goddam Okies in this town" (382). Despite these affronts and her insistence on sharing with the Wilsons over their protests, she still thinks primarily in terms of the family unit. Her reaction upon arriving in Bakersfield is "the fambly's here" (311), and in the encounter with the vigilantes she counsels Tom to do nothing because "the fambly's breakin' up" (381).

The first significant change in the family's attitude occurs in the Weedpatch government camp where the Wallaces share their work with Tom, although they may thereby cut their own meager earnings. The self-governing arrangement of the camp also makes the Joads feel like decent people again. Evaluating her recent experiences, Ma says, ". . . in Needles, that police. He done somepin to me, made me feel mean. Made me feel ashamed. An' now I ain't ashamed. These folks is our folks. . . . Why, I feel like people again" (420); but she prefaces her remarks with the reminder, "We're Joads," and she still talks about settling the family in a little white cottage. At this camp the Joads meet people who do not think of cooperation as "charity," but all is not harmonious even here. A religious bigot attacks Rose of Sharon, and the women of the camp stage a garbage fight. Pa Joad is still far from won over to Casy's way of thinking—"I can't starve so's you can get two bits," he tells another man in a quarrel about taking others' jobs for lower wages (463).

The easy atmosphere of the government camp, where—as one man observes—"We're all a-workin' together" (488), is in striking contrast to the tense atmosphere at the Hooper Ranch. There the prevailing attitudes are epitomized by a checker's remark that putting holes in the bottom of buckets "keeps people from stealing them" (506). Here Ma learns "one thing good"—"If you're in trouble or hurt or need—go to poor people. They're the only ones that'll help—the only ones" (513–14). The Joads still think of help, however, only as a means towards maintaining the family. When Casy, now a labor organizer, pleads with Tom to support a strike against the ranch, Tom replies, "Pa wouldn' do it. . . . He'd say it wasn't none of his business.... Think Pa's gonna give up his meat on account a other fellas?" (524).

A family crisis is precipitated at the ranch by Tom's impetuously killing the man who has killed Casy. Tom decides that he must run away because, as he tells Ma, he "can't go puttin' this on you folks." Ma retorts angrily, "... goin' away ain't gonna ease us. It's gonna bear us down.... They was the time when we was on the lan'. They was a boundary to us then.... We was always one thing—we was the fambly—kinda whole and clear. An' now we ain' clear no more.... We're crackin' up, Tom. There ain't no fambly now" (536). She pleads with him to stay, and the family leaves the ranch. Ma's suspicion of any idea beyond that of loyalty to the family appears in her replying, when Tom insists that he must go, "You can't.... They wouldn' be no way to hide out. You couldn' trus' nobody. But you can trus' us. We can hide you, an' we can see you get to eat while your face gets well" (545–46).

A major change in attitude has occurred, however, by the time of the final interview between Tom and Ma. Young Ruthie Joad has undone the family by boasting about it. In a childish quarrel, she has revealed that her brother is a killer who is hiding nearby. Ma realizes then that Tom must go. While hiding, Tom has been thinking over Casy's ideas; and, when his mother says that she is worried that she may not know what has become of her son he tells her:

"Well, maybe like Casy says, a fella ain't got a soul of his own, but on'y a piece of a big one—an' then.... Then it don' matter. Then I'll be all aroun' in the dark. I'll be ever'where—wherever you look. Wherever they's a fight so hungry people can eat, I'll be there.... An' when our folks eat the stuff they raise an' live in the houses they build—why, I'll be there" (572).

Tom has given up his concept of clan loyalty and has replaced it with the concept that one must help whoever needs help. Gradually the rest of the family comes to share this concept.

Pa learns the lesson of cooperation during the building of a dam to hold floodwater out of a cotton-pickers' camp; and he cries, "We can do her if ever'body helps" (595). Uncle John, too, finally breaks with tradition in order to teach the world a lesson. Instead of burying Rosasharn's stillborn baby, he sets it adrift in a creek, saying, "Go down in the street an' rot an' tell 'em that way. That's the way you can talk. Don' even know if you was a boy or girl. Ain't gonna find out" (609).

Most importantly, Ma's acceptance of the idea of a responsibility beyond the family after her last meeting with Tom is shown in her conversation with a neighbor whom she thanks for helping during Rosasharn's labor:

> The stout woman smiled, "No need to thank. Ever'body's in the same wagon. S'pose we was down. You'd give us a han'."
> "Yes," Ma said, "we would."
> "Or anybody."
> "Or anybody. Use' ta be the fambly was fust. It ain't so now. It's anybody. Worse off we get, the more we got to do." (606).

But while this speech accepts the spirit of Casy's idea of universal brotherhood, it does not translate the meaning into action. Some concluding gesture must indicate that education of the heart has transformed the family's behavior.

The opportunity arises in the barn where the family discovers the famished man. Ma's unstated suggestion that Rosasharn give her milk to him carries into practice the idea that "worse off we get, the more we got to do." Having come to the barn with almost nothing, the family, through Rosasharn, gives the one thing it has left to offer—the most intimate gift it could. The tableau in the barn does not halt an unfinished story; it marks the end of the story that Steinbeck had to tell about the Joads. Their education is complete; they have transcended familial prejudices. What happens to them now depends upon the ability of the rest of society to learn the lesson that the Joads have learned. The novel is neither riddle nor tragedy—it is an epic comedy of the triumph of the "holy spirit." The Joads have not been saved from physical privation, but they have saved themselves from spiritual bigotry.

The Grapes of Wrath is not, therefore, a period piece about a troublesome past era; it is an allegory applicable wherever prejudice and a proud sense of self-importance inhibit cooperation. The message of the novel is that cooperation can be achieved only when individuals of their own volition put aside special interests and work together to achieve a common purpose.

This message is not new in American literature. As Frederic Ives Carpenter pointed out not long after *The Grapes of Wrath* appeared, the novel reflects the thinking of the nineteenth-century American transcendentalists:

> Beside and beyond their function in the story, the ideas of John Steinbeck and Jim Casy possess a significance of their own. They continue, develop, integrate and realize the thought of great writers of American history. Here the mystical transcendentalism of Emerson reappears, and the earthy democracy of Whitman, and the pragmatic instrumentalism of William James and John Dewey.... Jim Casy translates American philosophy into words of one syllable, and the Joads translate it into action.[4]

Steinbeck's development of the vitally American thought of the transcendentalists does not indicate any specific "influence" of Emerson or Whitman. Neither Steinbeck nor Casy mention these past writers. Those who suppose that a younger man's ideas' paralleling and developing an older man's necessarily indicate a direct influence of the older on the younger make the very assumption that Emerson warned against—that we learn only from books. As Whitman suggested in "Song of Myself" two men may independently develop the same ideas from a sympathetic reading of Nature and observation of their fellowmen.

II *Structure and Meaning*

The danger always exists, however, that readers will become so involved in the fortunes of the particular characters in a novel that its universal implications will be overlooked. To avoid this danger that *The Grapes of Wrath* might be interpreted as a unique story of one family's history, Steinbeck paired the chapters carrying forward the history of the Joads with others that show the general implications of the things that happened specifically to them.

Although the author nowhere in *The Grapes of Wrath* discusses the method he is using, he explains—as Peter Lisca indicates in *The Wide World of John Steinbeck*—the conscious literary theory behind his procedure in his preface to a book containing still pictures from the film, *The Forgotten Village*, Steinbeck's next creative project after *The Grapes of Wrath*. Commenting upon the problems that had to be faced in making this film about the introduction of scientific medicine to a remote, superstition-ridden Mexican community, the novelist explained:

A great many documentary films have used the generalized method, that is, the showing of a condition or an event as it affects a group of people. . . . In *The Forgotten Village* we reversed the usual process. Our story centered on one family in one small village. We wished our audience to know this family very well, and incidentally to like it, as we did. Then, from association with this little personalized group, the larger conclusion concerning the racial group can be drawn with something like participation.[5]

In *The Grapes of Wrath*, Steinbeck did not take a chance on one method or the other; he used both to leave nothing undone that might help get his point across. The Joad story focuses, like *The Forgotten Village*, upon one family; and the "generalized method" is used in the interchapters. By using this double approach, Steinbeck did what he could to protect himself against the attacks some people made upon the book. By presenting the problems he was concerned with through the history of a particular family, he forced readers to visualize these problems as they affected individuals; and he denied escapists the consolation of the sociology textbook that treats depressed groups in numbers too large to be comprehended.

On the other hand, by using the generalized method, he denied in advance any charges that the history of the Joads was unique. By making what happened to the Joads representative of general situations that he also commented upon, he avoided the error made by some who attempted to answer his novel by presenting a unique case and suggesting that it was typical. In the device of the interchapter, Steinbeck found exactly the technique that he needed to make his novel simultaneously a general and an intensely personal history of the travails of a culture in transition.

Even this last description, however, too much limits the novel as a tale of a particular time and place. In a letter to his editor, Steinbeck observed that there are "five layers" in the book, although a reader finds no more than he has in himself. Steinbeck nowhere explains what "five layers" he has in mind, but an inquiry into his meaning might begin with the most famous explanation of "levels of meaning" in literature in Dante's *Convivio*:

Exposition must be *literal* and *allegorical*. And for the understanding of this you should know that writings can be understood and must be explained, for the most part, in four senses. One is called *literal*; and this is the one which extends not beyond the letter itself. The next is called *allegorical*; and this is the one which is hidden beneath the cloak of these fables, being a truth concealed under pretty fiction.... The third sense is called *moral*; and this is the one which readers must ever diligently observe in writings, for their own profit and for that of their pupils.... The fourth sense is called *anagogical*, or supersensual; and this is when we expound spiritually a writing which, even in the letter, through the very things exprest expresseth things concerning eternal glory.[6]

We have examined already the literal and the allegorical levels of the novel as the literal tale of the migration from Oklahoma and as an illustration of the "education of the heart." On the "moral level," as I have also already suggested, the author—like Dickens—is expressing outrage that such conditions exist and pleading with readers to play their role in alleviating and eliminating them; the novel demands not agreement, but action. On the anagogic level, as Dante puts it, a writing expresses things "concerning eternal glory," a radiant security beyond the chaotic flux of man's material experiences. Does Tom Joad achieve a vision of such glory when he tells Ma that he'll "be all aroun' in the dark"? Does he urge the reader to aspire to a similar vision? Here the novel, with its rejection of traditional religious solutions, may provoke most thoughtful controversy.

Steinbeck speaks of a fifth layer. May individuality be transcended altogether? What of the "one big soul" that Casy feels everybody may be part of? What does Steinbeck mean when he speaks in chapter 14 of "Manself"? Are these concepts related to the "pure consciousness" sought through some meditation techniques? Is there a "layer" of experience at which individual distinctions are obliterated and at which life is perceived only as an all-pervasive force?

Contemplated in this manner, *The Grapes of Wrath* is not just a story of the Okies' migration to California, of man's perpetual pursuit of an elusive dream, of man's injustices to man, or even of the final reward of the deserving—the pure in heart that shall see God. It is rather the endless story of the strivings of a life-force to endure and triumph over inert obstacles that beset its way.

CHAPTER 7

Dramas of Consciousness—The War Years

TWICE in his fiction Steinbeck paraphrases Christ's words on the cross. Both speakers are "red" labor agitators:

> "It's all for you. We're doing it for you. All of it. You don't know what you're doing!" ("The Raid," [1934]).
> "Listen. . . . You fellas don' know what you're doin'. You're helpin' to starve kids." (Casy in *The Grapes of Wrath*, [1939], p. 527).

The difference between the two contexts is that the young organizers in "The Raid" also don't know what they are doing; however, Casy knows exactly what he is doing, and he manages before he dies to translate his illumination to Tom Joad. Root in "The Raid" has vaguely Christian sentiments, but his more hardened Communist partner warns against them. Casy has rejected institutional Christianity, but he has evolved his own kind of rejuvenated faith: "I figgered about the Holy Sperit and the Jesus Road. I figgered, 'Why do we got to hang it on God or Jesus? Maybe,' I figgered, 'maybe it's all men an' all women we love. . . .' "

The sentiment is religious. Any concept of universal love commits man to faith in something that cannot be materially "proved." Actually, the attackers in "The Raid" do know on a superficial level what they are doing; they are striking down an obstacle that annoys them as wanton boys might swat a fly. They have no comprehension, however, of the long-range consequences of their actions. Mac in *In Dubious Battle* understands their motives: "To some of these guys property's more important than their lives." But although Mac—like Thoreau—can see through the folly of seeking security in property, he makes the destructive mistake of putting a "cause" before his relationship to another person. He has not really examined his own motives. When Jim challenges him, "You protect me all the time, Mac. And sometimes I get the feeling you're not protecting me for the Party, but for yourself," Mac can only reply with an angry outburst that precludes their achieving any rapport with each other's consciousness beyond that provided by mutual adherence to a partisan program. They have not progressed beyond what Joseph Conrad's Marlow in *Heart of Darkness* calls "principles" to "a deliberate belief"; therefore, they are doomed to the fate of Conrad's Kurtz.

The heroes of Steinbeck's works beginning with *The Grapes of Wrath*, however, are willing to live—or, if necessary, to die—for their people in the full knowledge of what they are doing. They battle the enemies of superstition, fear of the unknown, and tyranny with a deliberate belief that they discover within themselves—not with principles institutionally imposed upon them.

Understandably exhausted by his work on *The Grapes of Wrath* and the emotional disturbances resulting from both the great success of the novel and the attacks upon it, Steinbeck did not move at once to another large project; he turned instead to a quartet of short and greatly diversified works. The earliest conceived was "The Log" from *The Sea of Cortez*, which first appeared in an elaborately illustrated catalogue of marine specimens that Steinbeck and Ed Ricketts collected on an expedition to the Gulf of California, but that was subsequently printed separately after Ricketts's death with a preliminary tribute by Steinbeck, "About Ed Ricketts." The relationship of the nonteleological thinking discussed in this "Log" to Steinbeck's fiction has been extensively discussed, but it is difficult to treat "The Log" as representative of Steinbeck's thought; indeed, recent research by Richard Astro has established that the philosophy is primarily Ricketts's.[1]

The next three works, however, constitute a kind of verbal triptych, but they have not previously been examined as such because of their great differences in form and even in medium. *The Forgotten Village* is a documentary film, though the narrated sound track has been published with stills from the film; *The Moon Is Down* is the second and most controversial of Steinbeck's play-novelettes; and the third, *Bombs Away* is a propaganda piece that was commissioned by the United States Army Air Force to explain the role of its bombing crews in the American war effort.

These works are not, however, so varied as they first appear; an analysis of the similarities between them helps clarify some misapprehensions that have developed from considering them in isolation. All three are propaganda; and, even more important, but less noted, all three are works of fiction, basically novelettes. Finally, all three celebrate the triumph of the man who achieves self-liberation and who also promises to contribute to the liberation of his people by breaking through social conventions and private dreams to develop a self-conscious identity as part of a team that is working toward a common goal.

I The Forgotten Village (1941)

Steinbeck and a film crew headed by Herbert Kline (recently returned from Europe where he had risked his life filming *Lights Out in Europe,* an on-the-spot record of the German occupation of Poland) went to Mexico to make a film about a possible Fascist threat to the country—a film that might have much resembled *In Dubious Battle,* which pessimistically and objectively portrays the triumph of bigotry and accompanying violence over "little people's" dreams of the good life. But, though Fascistic landowners appear briefly in the film, the villain becomes the village's *curandera* ("Wise Woman") and the enemy, superstition. The hero, Juan Diego, resolves at the end to become not a political organizer but a doctor. After the narrator concludes that "The change will come, is coming, as surely as there are thousands of Juan Diegos in the villages of Mexico," the boy's self-conscious last word shows his recognition and acceptance of the role that he must play as "leader of the people," not toward the fulfillment of some political vision, but toward better health that may provide a solid foundation for the realization of individual dreams.

The significance of the boy's choice is pointed out by a soldier he meets on the way to the city: "Yours is the true people's work . . . saving, not killing; growing, not dying." Juan Diego is thrown out of his father's house for siding with the scientists; but Steinbeck affirms that the future is on the boy's side. "The old and new meet and sometimes clash," the narrator begins, "but from the meetings a gradual change is taking place in the villages." The old people are reluctant to surrender their past and their power; but, as the film concludes, the young will slowly and patiently change things. Although shot on location in a Mexican village with native actors, the work is fiction: Juan Diego plays not himself, but an apotheosis of militant youth. The setting is Mexican, but the sentiments are Steinbeck's.

II   The Moon Is Down (1942)

The situation in *The Moon Is Down* is remarkably similar to that in the film: the too trusting people of a small, invaded village have been betrayed. They are victims not of physical disease spread by germs from a well but of the psychic disease of a power-mad dictator. Again, however, the young people escape the village to launch from afar the fight against the invader. Instead of breaking the villagers' spirits, the conquerors have jolted them out of their complacency—"the flies have conquered the flypaper," as one of the disturbed young conquering officers observes, thereby inadvertently providing a rallying cry for the people whom he has contemptuously supposed to be easy victims.

The difference between the stories is that the older people, the "wise men" of the conquered community in *The Moon Is Down*—the mayor and the doctor—are on the side of the young and sacrifice themselves in order to buy the time that the young people need to take effective action against the invaders. When Mayor Orden goes to his death, he is not bewildered and beaten, like Danny in *Tortilla Flat* or like Jim in *In Dubious Battle*; he is fully conscious of the choice that he has made in the cause of freedom.

The publication of the novel and the opening of the play version on Broadway in April, 1942, unleashed a flood of often venomous criticism of Steinbeck for being too soft on the invaders in the work. Peter Lisca describes in *The Wide World of John Steinbeck* (pages 186–88) the protracted controversy, particularly in the pages of the *New Republic*.

The furor is hard to understand today because, as Richard Astro points out, the work is neither a war story nor an antiwar story, but "a quasi-fictional philosophical debate, cut off by definition from World War II or any other war."[2] Part of the trouble was that after *The Grapes of Wrath*, any modest, dispassionate work would have been a letdown to Steinbeck's admirers, who expected him to reply to the plight of the occupied nations of Europe with the same militancy with which he had replied to the plight of the migrant workers in his native California. As Peter Lisca concludes, however, "It is now clear that the real critical issues were hopelessly entangled in the psychology of the war effort."[3] Still stunned and outraged by the surprise attack on Pearl Harbor, American audiences early in 1942 were in no mood to debate calmly the issues of tyranny and freedom.

Far from being soft on the invaders, as critics like James Thurber maintained, *The Moon Is Down* really suggests that the products of totalitarian regimes like those in Nazi Germany and Japan would soon crack under unexpected psychological pressure, while free men, when put to the test, would quickly develop the resourcefulness and self-reliance to triumph over their oppressors. This coolly optimistic work was, however, too controlled and intellectual for audiences that wanted violent action and strident denunciation as an outlet for national feelings of frustration.

European readers have admired the work, and their regard has been vindicated in the long run. Things did work out, after all, as Steinbeck prophesied in his heroic allegory; but his own optimism was later shattered by his experiences as a correspondent in the war zone. His much debated strategy in refusing to identify Germany and Norway by name has proved finally advantageous. One of the few speeches in the book that rings false today is Mayor Orden's comment to the commanding officer of the invading troops: "In all the world yours is the only government and people with a record of defeat after defeat for centuries and every time because you did not understand people." The very indefiniteness of the setting gives the work today, however, a value that could hardly have been suspected at the time that it appeared; for Steinbeck's thesis that the invaders were a "time-minded" people has been vindicated. An invading corporal observes of the conquered people, "They're fools. That's why they lost so quickly. They can't plan the way we can." But the invader's plans prove inflexible, geared to the clocks. When the timetable falters, he is lost. When he does not have the reinforcements that allow him to maintain control of the situation, time is on the side of the invaded people who are learning from bitter experience and who are producing, as old leaders are destroyed, new ones who will finally frustrate what Mayor Orden calls "the one impossible job in the world"— "to break man's spirit permanently."

The Moon Is Down is a remarkably prophetic work that
has suffered too much from rehashings of the emotional reception at the time it first appeared when Americans were desperately seeking "pep talks"—not cool counsel to cultivate self-
discipline. What no one could have suspected during World
War II is that what was then regarded as an ephemeral and
not very successful piece of propaganda would be revived
thirty years later with more success than it originally enjoyed,
while works acclaimed at the time (like the film *Wake Island*)
would be completely forgotten.

Unfortunately, the mixed reception of the work (it did have
enthusiastic defenders even during the war) seems to have
rattled Steinbeck more than it should have. Perhaps he couldn't
really believe in his own prophecies; for, though he could
have a character say in *The Moon Is Down*, "One of the tendencies of the military mind and pattern is an inability to
learn, an inability to see beyond the killing which is its job,"
he assigns these sentiments to one of the conquerors.
Moreover, he flies in the face of them by glorifying military
teamwork in his next work, which proves exactly the kind
of "pep talk" he had refused earlier to deliver. While patriotic-
ally understandable, *Bombs Away* is artistically suspect.

III   Bombs Away: The Story of a Bomber Team

Written expressly for the United States Army Air Force,
Bombs Away, though offered as a reportorial account of the
training of a bomber crew, is no less a work of fiction than
The Grapes of Wrath or *The Moon Is Down*. Actually it is
organized in much the same manner as *The Grapes of Wrath*,
for excerpts from official government publications serve as
unpunctuated interchapters in Steinbeck's fable about the for-
mation of a bomber crew. The crew assembled is as surely
idealized as the Joad family; Steinbeck provides folksy names
and life histories that are as typically American as those Norman Mailer later provided for the members of the platoon
in *The Naked and the Dead*. *Bombs Away* even has a story
line: the men enjoy small triumphs and reverses that reach
an improbable dramatic climax when, on its first live practice
run, "our crew" spots and sinks an enemy submarine in the
Gulf of Mexico.

The "realism" of the tale is additionally undermined by

Steinbeck's tampering novelistically with one aspect of the kind of actual situation purportedly described. A bomber crew included four commissioned officers—pilot, copilot, bombardier, and navigator; but, though the position of copilot (indispensable on a plane of a bomber's size) is occasionally mentioned in passing, no name or history is provided for the copilot of the crew that the reader follows through training. A good reason for this seeming oversight is that too much attention to the copilot would have undermined a principal message that Steinbeck is trying to communicate through his story—that, though everyone wants to be a pilot, the other crew members are not those washed out of pilot training (a wartime rumor with good grounds for support), but men with special backgrounds and aptitudes that could contribute most to the team in a particular assignment. He then represents pilot, bombardier, and navigator as being trained and commissioned at about the same time before meeting to begin their combat career on the blandly named "Baby" (a real "Everyman's" aircraft—most bombers, like the famed "Memphis Belle," bore names that meant something personally to the pilot or crew).

Except in an extraordinary emergency, these posts would not have been assigned men trained simultaneously, though early in the war a copilot might have been about the same age and rank as the bombardier and the navigator. The pilot, however, would have been a higher-ranking officer with long experience and proved ability. The Army Air Force was not entrusting its most expensive equipment to brand-new second lieutenants. The requirements of appealing fiction rather than hard fact shaped, therefore, the plotting of *Bombs Away*.

The essentially allegorical nature of this ostensibly journalistic work established, we can see its contribution to Steinbeck's triptych of man's consciously accepting his destiny. In the introductory chapter, the author sets forth the same concept of democratic man that he began to formulate in *The Grapes of Wrath* and that he presented argumentatively in that novel, in *The Forgotten Village*, and in *The Moon Is Down:*

Young men coming out of the schools, finding no jobs, no goals, became first despondent and then cynical; a curious and muscling state of mind which was considered intellectual despair, but which was actually the product of mental and physical idleness, descended

upon the youth of the country.... An antidote for the poisons of
this idleness and indirection might eventually have been found, some
great building program for the betterment of the country.... But
meanwhile, with one set of certainties gone and no new set established, the country floundered about... so convincingly that our
enemies considered us to be in a dying condition.... In attacking
us they destroyed their greatest ally, our sluggishness, our selfishness,
and our disunity.[4]

Although slight changes would be needed in the explanation
of the background, the final sentences apply exactly to the
situation in *The Moon Is Down.* By substituting exploitative
landholders and their traditional allies in oppressing little
people for the Axis powers, the statement fits equally well
The Grapes of Wrath and *The Forgotten Village,* as well as
the later *Pearl.* What had happened to Steinbeck in 1938 when
he began to convert "L'Affaire Lettuceberg" into *The Grapes
of Wrath* is that he had become convinced—long before the
events of World War II supported his argument—that the force
of a dream of freedom could overcome the force of reaction
and that "Westering" was indeed still alive in a person if he
had the training, the expertise to advance—in Thoreau's words
—"confidently in the direction of his dream." Steinbeck would
then no longer have to rely on the hypnotic rhetoric that characters in *In Dubious Battle* and *Of Mice and Men* had substituted
for well-informed action.

Bombs Away may also be, despite its unpretentiousness,
the key to understanding the slow decline that began in the
artistic power of Steinbeck's work; for what he himself had
learned—the expertise that he had acquired—from this commissioned work is that art and craft are not easily distin-
guishable, that his awesome talent could be channeled into
the production of propaganda as well as into the embodiment
of his own vision. The "sincerity" of the work is not in question.
The author donated all proceeds from the book to the Air
Forces Aid Society Trust Fund, and there is no evidence that
he did not believe passionately in the cause of expediting
American victory that he hoped to aid by winning sympathizers
for our unprecedented bombing program. What is in question
is whether those "new certainties" that confused young men
may need to overcome their intellectual despair are beneficial
to the artist, or, whether—to use Steinbeck's own phrase from

The Grapes of Wrath—the artist must not keep always "stumbling forward." In *Bombs Away!* Steinbeck actually puts on the blinders that his Doc Burton warns against in *In Dubious Battle:* the military preparedness of the Axis forces is a "bad" thing, but the galvanization of aimless young Americans into bombing crews is "good."

With *The Grapes of Wrath* Steinbeck had found what he had to say as an artist about his hopes for man. He had yet to give us—if he could—his portrait of a successful individual who is fully conscious of his identity, his capacities, and his limitations, who is seen, not like Casy and Tom Joad at the moment of their breakthrough to consciousness, but in his serene maturity. This he was to do in *Cannery Row*, a journey back to a freshly appreciated past. Beyond that his creation of dramas of consciousness would necessitate thematic repetition. *The Forgotten Village, The Moon Is Down*, and *Bombs Away* are indeed repetitions of part of the message of *The Grapes of Wrath* against new backdrops. The real shortcoming of all three of these technically expert works is that the artist had turned craftsman in order to do quickly and without fresh imagining what he already knew he could do well. Juan Diego, Mayor Orden, and the bomber crew that may live or die together have all learned the lesson of working together that Casy and Tom Joad have; but they have not progressed beyond the point that these earlier characters had reached.

For Steinbeck to strike out anew as an innovative artist in the post-World-War-II world, he was going to have to develop a new vision of a new era—not an easy thing for a middle-aged man much in the public eye to do. In one of the wisest pieces of self-analysis ever made public, Steinbeck told a reporter at the time his Nobel Prize was announced that it was not so easy to identify an underdog in the 1960s as it had been in the 1930s; one needed a new angle of vision. The suprising thing is not that, after *The Grapes of Wrath*, the hitherto restlessly experimental Steinbeck should have begun to repeat himself, but that in one final unassuming and still only partly appreciated work he could take the step needed to transform his vision of man's potential into an artistic embodiment of man's conscious transcendence of his imperfect world.

CHAPTER 8

Cannery Row *and Transcendent Man*

IN *Cannery Row*, as in *The Grapes of Wrath*, Steinbeck employs two complementary kinds of material, but the artful inter-reaction of the pieces of its intricate design have rarely been appreciated. The author maintained that this "poisoned cream-puff" was written on several levels of understanding and that people could take from it what they brought to it. Many readers, however, have not yet brought enough.

The book is disconcerting, to begin with, because it lacks a plot in any usual sense of the word. The plans of fellow residents of Monterey's Cannery Row to honor the proprietor of Western Biological Laboratory, Doc, with a party provides an organic framework; but the interpolated stories do not comment upon or make clear the immediate general implications of this meandering tale as do the interchapters in *The Grapes of Wrath*. We have to search for a subtler connection between the contrapuntal materials, bearing in mind the author's injunction in a prefatory chapter that perhaps the way to write this book might be "to open the page and let the stories crawl in themselves" in order to capture "the poem and the stink and the grating noise—the quality of light, the tone, the habit, and the dream" that comprise Cannery Row.

The chapters that carry forward what could be considered the main action (odd-numbered from 1 to 17, 18, 20; odd-numbered again from 21 to 29, 30 and 32) describe the hatching of the idea of a party to honor Doc, the first, disastrous party which Doc actually misses, and its disheartening aftermath, the rekindling of the festive spirit, and the successful second party. Rather than following the conventional pattern of an action rising through a series of episodes to a single climax—as in *Tortilla Flat*—the story follows (as is most fitting in a novel about a marine biologist who works in the tidal littoral) the pattern of a wave that grows slowly, hits a reef or barrier, divides and crashes prematurely, reforms, rises to a great height, and crashes at last with thunderous triumph on a beach.

Once discerned, the pattern is easy to trace in detail. The hint of a wave forms on the tranquil surface of life on Cannery Row when, at the end of the first chapter, Mack and the boys at the Palace Flophouse and Grill observe, "That Doc is a fine fellow. We ought to do something for him." By the end of chapter 5, the sentiment is shared by people along the Row: "Everyone who thought of [Doc] thought next, 'I really must do something nice for [him].' " This "something nice," however, is, like the Palace Flophouse itself, "no sudden development." In chapter 7, the desire to do something crystallizes into plans for a party; in chapter 9, the boys decide to raise money for the party by hunting frogs; and, in chapters 11, 13, and 15, the events of the frog-hunt occur in their none-too-smooth course. Between chapters 16 and 21, the design of the novel is flawed. Peter Lisca reports that the publishers dropped one interchapter—subsequently published elsewhere—from the novel;[1] and I suspect that it was from this section. Enough of the design remains, however, to make it appear that the wave divides at this point. In chapters 17 and 18, we follow Doc out of town on a collecting expedition; and, in chapters 20 and 21, we attend the party that the guest of honor misses, which results in the devastation of Doc's laboratory.

In chapter 23, the wave, which has been temporarily divided and smashed, reforms itself; and we are pushed rapidly forward toward the triumphant end of the novel. The recovery of the Palace Flophouse dog from distemper symbolizes a general lifting of a pall that has hung over the Row since the catastrophic party. When Dora, the Madame of the Bear Flag Restaurant, suggests that Mack repair the damages that the disastrous party caused by giving another party, which Doc attends, the temporarily dissipated energies of the community are refocused. Preparations for the party gather momentum in chapters 25 and 27; finally, in chapters 29 and 30, with a tremendous crescendo, the party itself occurs; and it ends with an explosive flourish as a twenty-five-foot string of firecrackers is lit.

In chapter 32, when the wave is crashed and spent, we find Doc alone clearing up the litter left in its wake, just as he often searches the tide pool after an ocean's wave retreats. He is reading—as he has at the party—from the Sanskrit lyric

"Black Marigolds." This conclusion has provoked speculation, since the narrative itself ends when Doc finishes cleaning up after the party, wipes his hands, and turns off the record player. Something beyond the ending of the story is added through the last pages; but, to learn what, we must first examine the interchapters.

The contrast between the central narrative and the inter-polated tale is less clear in *Cannery Row* than in *The Grapes of Wrath*, for Steinbeck makes little use of interchapters for editorializing, and the interchapters sometimes involve charac-ters from the central story. I believe, however, that a closer correlation than has usually been acknowledged may be found between the two parts of the book and that we can demonstrate that most interchapters are "associated" with the chapters in the main narrative that they follow and that these paired chap-ters reinforce each other in suggesting some single point.

The clue to the purpose of the interchapters may be found in chapter 2, the first of them, in which the author writes, "The word is a symbol." "The word," he continues, as he comments on characters introduced in the first chapter, "sucks up Cannery Row, digests it, and spews it out. . . . Lee Chong is more than a Chinese grocer. He must be. Perhaps he is evil balanced and held suspended by good. . . ." The purpose of this comment—as of the next one, in which Mack and the Palace Flophouse boys are described as "the Virtues, the Graces, the Beauties of the hurried mangled craziness of Mon-terey and the cosmic Monterey"—is to alert the reader to follow the story not merely as an arch narrative about a collection of eccentrics, but as an allegory: these characters are not just distinctive individuals in Monterey but symbols of "cosmic" tendencies as seen through Emerson's "transparent eyeball." Certainly if any author has ever granted us license to read his novel as an allegory and to search for symbolic interrelation-ships between the one long narrative and the many interwoven short narratives, Steinbeck has here.

In chapters 3 and 4, the note of tragedy that increases in intensity and then is gradually tempered is sounded. Readers who carry away the impression that *Cannery Row* is a "funny book" do so because of the overpowering strength of the descriptions of the parties near the end; the reader who stopped reading, however, at the end of the fourth chapter would probably find the book profoundly depressing. The third chapter introduces Dora and the noble prostitutes of the Bear Flag; but it concentrates on the story of William, the establishment's former bouncer, who commits suicide when the tight society of Cannery Row laughs at and rejects him.

The fourth chapter is a cryptic account of an old Chinaman who daily makes his inscrutable way through the Row. Most people fear him, but one brave boy who makes fun of him is repaid with a vision that makes him whimper. The old man means various things to different people, but his basic characteristic is his utter detachment from the world around him—a separation that old people interpret as death, young people as loneliness. The old Chinaman symbolizes the terrors of isolation to those who rely most upon the opinion of the world around them, rather than upon their internal resources, for happiness.

These chapters are related in two ways: both are "essays in loneliness"—as Ed Ricketts, the model for Doc, said the novel as a whole was; and both concern people who have either the actual experience or the frightening vision of being isolated from the world. The chapters are also more specifically linked by the motivations of the principal characters. William, the bouncer in chapter 3, commits suicide when he realizes that, since he has finally impressed someone that he will, he must, even though it now seems silly to do so. Similarly, Andy, the boy who is really the main character in chapter 4—the old Chinaman is simply the vehicle that provides Andy's experience—taunts the old man to "keep his self-respect." Both incidents illustrate that a person may be driven to frightening and even self-destructive actions to maintain an image.

The next two chapters introduce Doc, but the relationship between them is quite different from that between the previous pair. Chapter 5 generalizes about Doc, and chapter 6 demonstrates his characteristics in specific situations. The main point of chapter 5 is that Doc's "mind had no horizon—and his sympathy had no warp." In the next chapter, this lack of bias—as well as the contrast between Doc and the more limited characters—is demonstrated when Doc tells Hazel, one of Mack's boys, that he thinks stinkbugs keep their tails in the air because they are praying: "If we did something as inexplicable and strange, we'd probably be praying." "Let's get the hell out of here" is the only reply from his good-natured but simpleminded companion, who is unable to cope with analogical thinking or with shockingly unprecedented ideas.

An attack on respectability—always one of Steinbeck's principal targets—begins on a muted note in the next pair of chapters. In chapter 7, we learn that Mack and the boys have their own code of behavior. When it is suggested that they work in a cannery to earn a few dollars to give a party for Doc, Mack rejects the idea: "We got good reputations and we don't want to spoil them. Every one of us keeps a job for a month or more when we take one. That's why we can always get a job when we need one." These "bums" have standards, but they are the masters, not the slaves, of them. In the droll eighth chapter, we see the other side of the coin; for, when Sam Malloy becomes a "landlord" by renting out large abandoned pipes as sleeping rooms, his wife is overwhelmed by a longing for respectability that finally crystallizes into a desire for curtains, despite the absence of windows in the old boiler, the Malloys' home. When her husband tells her that he does not "begrutch" her the curtains, but that they have no use for them, she sobs, "Men just don't understand how a woman feels." Her reply indicates how standards of respectability enslave persons.

In the next two chapters (9 and 10), Doc is further characterized. Although his mind has no horizons, nature has placed physical limitations on all men. We learn also that he is not a sentimental optimist; he has no illusions about people. Having been victimized before, Doc is suspicious of such schemes of Mack's as a proposed trip to collect turtles. He is also, like all men, powerless in the face of nature's mistakes; for, in one of the most moving chapters in the novel, the tenth, Steinbeck recapitulates the story of George and Lennie in *Of Mice and Men* in his portrayal of the relationship between Doc and Frankie. Frankie, like Lennie, is one of nature's anomalies; he is unable to learn, and there is "something a little wrong with his coordination." Doc shows the boy the first affection he has known and does all in his power to aid him; but, when Frankie's coordination fails, Doc realizes that nothing can be done and refuses to take refuge—like George—in a hopeless dream. Doc is no neighborhood god; he is the best that imperfect man can hope to be in an imperfect universe, but he consciously learns and accepts his limitations.

In the next pair of chapters (11 and 12), the tempo of the novel accelerates as Steinbeck renews his attack on respectability. The twelfth chapter is a wry tale of proper citizens' insistence that the discarded "innards" of the famous humorist Josh Billings be given the same decent interment as his embalmed carcass—a savage burlesque of ignorance and literal-mindedness. This episode does not at first seem related to the preceding chapter about the Palace Flophouse boys' difficulties in fixing a truck that they borrowed for a frog hunt. The two chapters are, however, closely connected by brief passages in each: both burlesque respectable persons' suspicions of innovations that will ultimately change their culture, and the eleventh chapter comments that, as a result of the Model T Ford, "the theory of the Anglo-Saxon home became so warped that it never quite recovered"; the twelfth notes the resistance to the embalming of bodies when it was first practiced on the grounds that "it was sacrilegious since there was no provision for it in any sacred volume." These jibes made, Steinbeck again contrasts Mack's band with the respectable citizenry to the detriment of the latter: he calls Gay, the mechanic with a special gift for creatures of progress, "the little mechanic of God, the St. Francis of all things that turn and twist and explode," and he ridicules the "stern men" who oblige the undertaker to retrieve Billings's "tripas" and "wash them reverently."

The connection between the next two chapters is more immediately apparent. Just as the ninth and tenth chapters have recapitulated the situation in *Of Mice and Men*, the thirteenth and fourteenth present in capsule form the theme of *Tortilla Flat*—possession of property takes the fun out of life. In chapter 13, Mack and the boys become trespassers during a frog hunt. "The land's posted," the owner almost hysterically yells at them. "No fishing, hunting, fires, camping. Now you just pack up and put that fire out and get off this land." Mack's solicitous attentions to the owner's dog, however, mellow the man; but the point of the episode is made at the end of the chapter when Hazel—amazed at Mack's diplomatic skill—observes that Mack could have been President if he had so desired, and another observes, "There wouldn't be no fun in that." The owner of the land has not been having fun; nor has the watchman of the private beach at the Hopkins Marine Station, where the brief action of the fourteenth chapter occurs. When he yells at some soldiers and their girls, "You got to get off. This is private property!" a soldier simply replies, "Why don't you take a flying fuggut the moon." Obsession with property and prohibitions destroys joy and human sympathy.

The fifteenth and sixteenth chapters present another contrast —one between two women. In chapter 15, Mack and the boys visit the home of the man they have befriended and discover that his wife, a paragon of respectability, has been elected to the Assembly and is away making speeches when the legislature isn't in session. In thus serving the public by promoting herself, she ignores domestic duties. Steinbeck characterizes the type: "The kind of women who put papers on shelves and had little towels ... instinctively distrusted and disliked Mack and the boys. Such women knew that they were the worst threats to a home, for they offered ease and thought and companionship as opposed to neatness, order, and properness." In chapter 16, Steinbeck presents a contrasting picture of Dora, keeper of a bawdy house, who assumes responsibility for the care of the whole community during an influenza epidemic, even though it comes at a bad time for her own business. Paired, the two chapters present a telling contrast between selfish respectability and altruistic disreputability.

The next six chapters (17–22) present an organizational problem. As the book stands it is most satisfactory to read chapters 17 and 18 as a continuous narrative, chapter 19 as the commenting interchapter, chapters 20 and 21 as another continuous narrative, with chapter 22 as the summarizing interchapter. My guess, however, is that the omitted interchapter—published separately as "The Time the Wolves Ate the Vice-Principal"—should follow the present chapter 18 and that the present chapter 19 should be placed between chapters 17 and 18.

These last-mentioned chapters are the only two in which the action moves away from Monterey, for we follow Doc on a collecting trip to La Jolla. The change of scene is required to get Doc out of town during the first party. Chapter 17 is principally about Doc's love of truth, his discovery that his is not a general love, and his resorting to subterfuge to protect his privacy because people are suspicious of honest communications. An interchapter seems necessary after this chapter, but instead we plunge into chapter 18, which describes Doc's discovery at low tide in La Jolla of the body of a dead girl in an underwater rock crevice.

The present chapter 19 could belong after the present chapter 17 because the flagpole-skating incident discussed in detail in chapter 19 is mentioned in chapter 17 and both comment caustically on people's morbid curiosity. Chapter 17 points out that people trust those who do odd things to make money but that they distrust those who forgo financial gain in order to do what they like. Chapter 19 shows the profit motive at work as the curiosity about the flagpole-skater increases department-store sales and indicates the kind of prurient questions that people long to ask those who may find artistic satisfaction in a difficult feat—even in something as bizarre as flagpole skating.

The present chapter 18 develops the point about people's depraved curiosity. When Doc tells an inhabitant of the region that he is visiting about the dead girl, all the listener wishes to know is whether the body was "rotten or eat up." Although he has lived in this region all his life, he has never known that octopi are there because, as Doc tells him, "You've got to look for them."

The attack on money-mindedness and gross insensitivity that has been building through all three chapters is climaxed in the omitted interchapter. Since this tale is one of Steinbeck's most gruesome ones, I suspect publishers omitted it not as irrelevant but as too grisly for American readers who like to hear about death only when they have not been responsible for it. The chapter tells of the gathering of a pack of wolves on the Salinas courthouse lawn, their ranging about the town, and their finally eating the ailing vice-principal of the local high school on the steps of the house of a woman who sleeps through the episode. Like chapter 18, it emphasizes people's ignorance of what is happening on their own doorsteps. The idea that wolves range while the town sleeps also has implications that extend far beyond Salinas and relate to the general themes of the novel. Here Steinbeck makes one of his most memorable comments on the complacent attitude that

facilitated the development of the conditions that resulted in
World War II. We wonder, furthermore, if there is not particular
irony in the wolves' gathering at the courthouse and then eating
an educator. Whether or not Steinbeck intends a specific attack
on political anti-intellectualism or not, the chapter definitely
should be restored to the book as the capstone to Steinbeck's
attack on respectable society's insensitivity to the truth about
what's happening and its complacent complicity in unchecked
violence.

Chapters 20 and 21 are really a single long description of
the failure of the first party, just as chapters 29 and 30 are
of the success of the second; therefore, it seems appropriate
that these paired accounts should not be interrupted by
interchapters. The catastrophic affair described in chapters
20 and 21 casts a pall over Cannery Row. We have the first
indication that its residents have not always led happy lives
when Mack, dipping back into his past for the only time in
the novel, reveals that his life on the Row is not so much
a triumph of uninhibited individualism as an admission that
his life has been haunted by failure. "Ever'thing I done turned
sour," he tells Doc, explaining that he was once married: "If
I done a good thing it got poisoned up some way. If I give
her a present they was something wrong with it. She only
got hurt from me.... Same thing ever' place 'til I just got
to clowning. I don't do nothin' but clown no more. Try to
make the boys laugh."

A dark side exists in bohemian life: its joys are intense but
short-lived. Exactly the same point is made in chapter 22 about
Henri, the painter who devotes his life to building a boat
that he does not want to finish. Like Mack, Henri has been
successful on the Row; many women have shared his boat;
but all have left for the same reason: "They definitely felt
the need of a toilet." Again women—except for Dora's girls
—seem unable to adjust to the life of Cannery Row. The
difference between Mack and Henri is that Mack—like
Doc—has consciously appraised the situation and decided to
adjust to it; but the painter is continually frustrated by his
inability to decide what he really wants. Another contrast
between the main chapters and the interchapters is that the
former feature principally characters who participate in a continuing drama of consciousness and the latter often present

fleeting pictures of characters caught helplessly in Naturalistic tragedies like those described in many of Steinbeck's earlier writings. In this novel, Steinbeck fully contrasts for the first time what I have been calling *Naturalistic* characters and *self-conscious* characters; and he reveals his own new vision by steadily spotlighting the self-conscious ones and by giving them the last word.

Chapters 23 and 24 concern the turning of defeat into victory; and, like the two preceding ones, they repeat a point to stress its importance: that a person's confidence can be restored by gaining a sense of having successfully done something useful. In Chapter 23, Mack and the boys, crushed by the failure of their party, have their spirits revived when the grave illness of their dog at last gives them "something to do" and when their ministrations restore the pup to health. Similarly, when Tom Talbot's situation in chapter 24 seems hopeless and his wife Mary's seemingly irrepressible spirits fail to cheer him, he takes over when she is incapable of dealing with a cat that is destroying a mouse and this act removes the lines from his forehead.

In the next pair of chapters (25, 26), Steinbeck abruptly changes technique to provide not reinforcing but contrasting incidents, like those in chapters 11 and 12. Both chapters 25 and 26 deal with human resourcefulness in satisfying not physical but psychical wants. In chapter 25, this resourcefulness is used constructively when Mack devises and executes an elaborate scheme to discover Doc's birth date without revealing that a birthday party is being planned. In chapter 26, on the other hand, the cheerfulness of the last few chapters is temporarily dispelled by a grim picture of the way in which a clever but bored boy cruelly baits the weaker son of a suicide in order to create some "excitement" for himself. The viciousness of undisciplined physical and intellectual strength has rarely been so bitterly condemned as in this brief, almost entirely conversational interlude which illustrates Merlin's observation in *Cup of Gold* that those who think childhood a pleasure have forgotten their own.

Matters by this time are moving rapidly toward a climax. The next two chapters (27, 28), like the ninth and tenth ones, serve to remind us that limits exist upon the ability of even the most able. These chapters also diffuse the black-and-white contrast created by the preceding two by showing that love does not always bring joy and that pain does not result only from spite. Both chapters 27 and 28 show how people may suffer because of those they love. Doc, learning of the plans for the party in his honor, feels "great warmth," but he "quakes inwardly" because "he knew he would have trouble at the bank at the first of the month." He realizes that, if three or four such parties occur, he will lose the laboratory. His trouble is not only, however, that his friends' affection is costly; he suffers a more dispiriting difficulty when Frankie, learning of the party, steals a clock to give Doc. When told that the court thinks that Frankie had better be "put away," Doc realizes that the situation is hopeless. On the eve of the party to honor him, he suffers one of his most affecting losses.

The pattern of the novel changes slightly as it ends because one interchapter precedes the chapter with which it pairs, to enable the book to end on a note of affirmation. Before this pair of chapters, we have been carried in chapters 29 and 30 with breathtaking rapidity through the events of the day of the successful party. Having reached the climax of his main story, Steinbeck dispenses with allegory—except for making brief preparation for the concluding chapter by having Doc read from the Sanskrit poem "Black Marigolds." Steinbeck is intent here simply on describing the delightful air of anticipation and the subsequent overflow of spirits when people settle down at last to having a good time. It would be impertinent to interrupt this saturnalia with an edifying tale.

If *Cannery Row* were simply an escapist novel about the outrageous behavior of jovial pariahs, it would surely end with the fireworks that end the party. But, after the party is over, two more chapters lift this novel from the realm of diverting local-color stories and place it among those works that make a profound comment on the unique but possibly triumphant loneliness of the human condition. Indeed, a far closer relationship between the last two chapters exists than is at first evident, but their full significance can be appreciated only when they are considered together. The next-to-last chapter concerns a gopher who finds a secure home but no mate; therefore, he is compelled to move back into dangerous territory for female companionship—obviously a wry commentary on the difficulty of combining security and affection. This incident can be misread, however, if it is accepted as simply the same kind of "beast fable" as the allegory of the land turtle in chapter 3 of *The Grapes of Wrath*, which it superficially resembles.

Steinbeck has been sometimes criticized for treating men as if they were no different from other animals; but precisely what he is attempting to do in the last two chapters of *Cannery Row* is to distinguish man from the other animals—to indicate that man has unique capabilities if he will but cultivate them. The gopher in chapter 31 is a gopher, and the point of his dolorous tale is that the creature that lives by physical sensation must sacrifice security to the satisfaction of such desires—ones that probably doom him. If Steinbeck had thought, however, that this principle necessarily applied to man, *Cannery Row* would end here.

The last chapter is one of Steinbeck's most cryptic compositions, but comparison with the preceding chapter suggests an interpretation. After Doc finishes cleaning up the leavings of the party, he reads aloud to himself from "Black Marigolds" a section concluding with a verse that begins, "Even now/I know that I have savored the hot taste of life." As he reads, "white rats scampered and scrambled in their cages"; and rattlesnakes "lay still and stared into space with their dusty frowning eyes." This final contrast suggests that man is not like other animals; he is different because he has the unique capacity, celebrated in the poem, to preserve and even to re-create his experiences. He need not live a day-to-day existence only or forfeit security for physical affection as the gopher must. Only man has "savored the hot taste of life"; and, even if he has done so "just for a small and forgotten time," the recollection remains; as a result, he can live on the strength of memories preserved in works of art.

"Black Marigolds" is introduced, therefore, into the final chapters of Cannery Row not just because of what it says but because of what it is—a symbol of man's highest achievement. Ultimately, the novel is about the man who has learned with the assistance of art to triumph over his immediate sensations and surroundings, to move from Monterey to "the cosmic Monterey." In contrast to Doc, William, the bouncer in chapter 3, is like the gopher—he is an animal without internal resources who, deprived of affection, must set about his own destruction. Doc, the man who survives, is not perfect; but he seeks perfectibility. He has learned to find compensation for the frailties of human nature and other aspects of a physically imperfect universe in what William Butler Yeats calls "monuments of unaging intellect." Doc is one of those few "wisest," whom Walter Pater celebrates, who spend their mortal interval in "art and song."

The novel is, therefore, a defense of poetry—Steinbeck's answer to the challenge of the horror of war. *Cannery Row* is not a novel about a physical battle against a transient enemy to make life possible; it is a tribute to the intellectual struggle of the disciplined consciousness against the enemies of ignorance and unthinking respectability in order to make life worthwhile. At the time of his extreme disheartenment with what he had seen of war, Steinbeck sought his own escape into sanity by devising an allegory that would share with others his concept of the highest human potential for coming to terms with life through art.

CHAPTER 9

Dramas of Consciousness—
The Search for a Natural Saint

I have argued that the three short works immediately preceding *Cannery Row* constitute a triptych about the "committed man" who develops a conscious responsibility for his own behavior coupled with a conscience that is at the service of his people. Although *The Forgotten Village, The Moon Is Down,* and *Bombs Away* are thin and overly schematic, they are strikingly accurate prophecies that display Steinbeck's talent for combining undistorted perception with a conversational narrative style, one that deals so serenely with issues often approached hysterically that readers suffering from wartime pressures frequently missed the understated points. Then in *Cannery Row* Steinbeck capped his portrayal of man's slow metamorphosis from victim to victor with a remarkable tribute to his friend Ed Ricketts in the portrait of Doc, who at last finds in the contemplation of art a personal peace of mind that enables him to transcend the limitations of imperfect nature that Steinbeck had portrayed years earlier in *The Red Pony.*

Having achieved such a picture of man's ultimate potential, Steinbeck faced the problem of repeating himself unless his vision underwent another change of the kind that led him, while composing *The Grapes of Wrath,* from Naturalism to the drama of consciousness. He seemed temperamentally incapable of exact repetition; yet he would not retreat from a hard-won vision of the possible triumph of conscious man until very near the end of his life when a streak—but even then only a small one—of cynicism appears in *The Winter of Our Discontent,* his last novel.

Not surprisingly, Steinbeck turned more and more to journalism, as Norman Mailer later did when he reached a similar block in his development as a novelist. Steinbeck also continued, however, to write fiction; and in the seven years between the publications of *Cannery Row* (1945) and *East of Eden* (1952), he published three short and not very satisfactory fictions—*The Pearl* (1947), *The Wayward Bus* (1947), and *Burning Bright* (1950)—that constitute a second triptych. Like the earlier trio, these works are well designed; but the style of the writing is strained and artificial, and the tone of the books is strident and pontifical. Like Sinclair Lewis's work after *Dodsworth* (1929), Steinbeck's post-World-War-II novels are less admirable than his earlier ones because of the shrillness of his language and some unprecedented lapses in taste in diction and plotting.

These next works do not deal—as the wartime fictions had —with the conscious problems of commitment to an ideal; instead they explore the role of love, especially familial love, in the "examined life." All three spring from a search for a hero—a person who has the characteristics of the classically trained Mayor Orden in *The Moon Is Down* or the college-graduate doctors in *The Forgotten Village* and air-force officers in *Bombs Away,* but who will emerge from among the "little people" that had concerned Steinbeck from the beginning of his Naturalistic period through *The Grapes of Wrath.* Although this search to find a new kind of hero for a war-weary and disillusioned world is evident only in retrospect, *The Pearl, The Wayward Bus,* and *Burning Bright* (along with the film script for Elia Kazan's *Viva Zapata!*) constitute a quest for a folk saint whose triumphs might counterbalance the depressing defeats that "natural man" had suffered in *Tortilla Flat, In Dubious Battle,* and *Of Mice and Men.*

I   The Pearl *(1947)*

Of the three novels, *The Pearl* has been the most highly regarded because of its appealing characters, its obvious allegory, and its innocuous language that suits it for high-school literature programs; but both *The Wayward Bus* and *Burning Bright*—like most of the increasingly frank fiction written in the United States since World War II—deal with situations that raise questions that squeamish school administrators and vigilant parents wish avoided. An introductory statement suggests that *The Pearl* may be read as a parable, but it is one into which each person reads his own life and from which he takes his own meaning. In "John Steinbeck as Fabulist," Lawrence William Jones discusses Steinbeck's increasing penchant for parable in his postwar fiction and argues that the novelist had always been "hospitable to ready-made artistic structures and the various conventions of parable."[1]

Drawing on the distinctions that Sheldon Sacks makes in *Fiction and the Shape of Belief*, Jones maintains that a "novel" is a work "organized so that it introduces characters, about whose fates we are made to care, in unstable relationships which are then further complicated until the complication is finally resolved by the removal of the represented instability." This description fits very well most of Steinbeck's works of the 1930s up to *The Grapes of Wrath*. From the "novel," Jones, still quoting Sacks, distinguishes the "apologue," which includes the forms of fable, as "a fictional example of the truth of a formulable statement or a series of such statements."

In short, "parable nearly always gives the impression that its purpose is anterior, that it was written to embody a pre-existing formulable moral statement"; thus, "while the novelist usually is content to mimic the primary world . . . [,] the fabulist creates his own secondary world, more or less complete in itself."[2] Without subscribing entirely to this concept of novel and apologue, we can see that the problem which the parable writer faces is manifest in the seemingly casual phrase about a world "more or less complete in itself." As I have written in a discussion of Steinbeck in *American Winners of the Nobel Literary Prize*: " . . . if the writer-critic is to make a valid and useful criticism of society, he must create characters who are not individuals in quest of unique identities, but allegorical representatives of mankind as a whole. He must create a convincingly specific situation that mirrors a recognizably general one."[3] Steinbeck, I continue, "had quite uneven success in achieving this difficult fusion." *Cannery Row* is a triumph, but he began having trouble as early as *The Moon Is Down* and *Bombs Away*. The major difficulties, however, arose with *The Pearl*.

The story was not entirely Steinbeck's invention; for, in *The "Log" from "The Sea of Cortez,"* he reports hearing a story about an Indian boy's finding a great pearl that should have freed him from the necessity of ever working again. But the boy was so much beaten and tortured by would-be thieves that he finally cursed the pearl and threw it back into the sea.[4] The story that Steinbeck reports hearing is a perfect, self-contained parable that can be read in a variety of ways—it provides consolation for the unsuccessful, a pat on the back for those who choose freedom over wealth, and a scourging of the guilt of those who have suffered for choosing to serve Mammon. Steinbeck was not content, however, to leave well enough alone; for, although he said that he thought the legend was probably true, he found it "too reasonable" and began to tamper with it.

As a result, the fisherboy of the source, surely a "wise primitive," is transformed into Kino, an unwed father who hungers for respectability. He finds "the greatest pearl in the world"; but, after the brokers try to cheat him and he is harassed and tortured by would-be robbers and assassins, who do accidentally kill his child, he hands his wife the pearl to cast back into the sea. Kino's motives are quite different from the folk figure's, for the legendary boy—according to the report in *Sea of Cortez*—saw "in his one pearl . . . the ability to be drunk as long as he wished, to marry any one of a number of girls, and to make many more a little happy, too" and to purchase masses "to pop him out of Purgatory like a squeezed watermelon seed." Kino, on the other hand, sees the great pearl as providing the opportunity to pay for a church wedding, new clothes, a rifle, a schooling for his son—objectives that are far more understandable and acceptable than the original fisherboy's to the suburbanite readers of the *Woman's Home Companion*, where the story first appeared.

Although the setting remains Mexico, Steinbeck transferred the action to Levittown. Furthermore, getting rid of the pearl isn't even Kino's idea. Juana, his jittery common-law wife, begins nagging him to dispose of what has become his "soul" long before he agrees. Not until he has killed three men, seen his boat destroyed, and had his baby killed by his pursuers does he return the pearl to the sea. To stress the symbolic importance of these events, Steinbeck heavy-handedly relates each to one of three songs—of the Family, the Enemy, and the Pearl (capitals Steinbeck's)—that Kino keeps hearing in his head. Although we feel sorry for Kino, he has the makings of a stubborn, pompous, middle-class bore with a fretful American suburbanite wife. He is certainly a far cry from the ingratiating rascal of the legend. Also, whereas the original tale has a dreamlike wistfulness about its telling, *The Pearl* is studded with angry outbursts against social injustice that are incompatible with the improbability of the events. *The Pearl* sounds like a parable, but it isn't one, because it is not—as Sheldon Sacks insists a parable should be—more or less complete in itself.

The defect in *The Pearl* becomes apparent when we compare it with Ernest Hemingway's *The Old Man and the Sea* (1952), which is similarly based on a Latin-American fisherman's legend. Hemingway recounted the original tale in *Death in the Afternoon* (1932), and the only change he made in it when he converted it into a novel was to make his hero stoic and long-suffering instead of simply confused. However we interpret Hemingway's parable it is self-contained, for, after the sharks consume the great fish, the story ends. Steinbeck's *The Pearl*, however, remains too much of a "novel"—following Sacks's terms—to be a satisfactory "apologue." The narrative is by no means "more or less complete" because too many loose ends remain unresolved, as in real life. After the original fisherboy throws the pearl back into the sea, "He was a free man again with his soul in danger and his food and shelter insecure," but he's able to laugh "a great deal" about it, and disposal of the pearl ends the action. But Steinbeck's Kino has lost the boat that he needs to make his living, he has killed four men, and we certainly can't believe that he will ever laugh again. What is going to happen to him now? We are not told. Details like that can be left unresolved in a novel that shares real life's messiness, as Steinbeck leaves such details unresolved at the end of *The Grapes of Wrath*; but matters have to be resolved in a parable so that consistent interpretations from a variety of viewpoints can be made.

The popularity of *The Pearl* is actually a criticism of readers who want to admire Kino's final grand gesture of renunciation without considering the unresolved problems that have been raised by the action. Kino "had lost one world and had not gained another," Steinbeck observes at one point; but the grave implications of this remark are never explored. The conclusion of the novel leaves the impression that Kino is returning to his old life as the surviving characters did in the novels Steinbeck had written in the 1930s, like *Tortilla Flat* and *Of Mice and Men*, but these were stories about victims of a world they had not made and could not understand. Steinbeck is trying in *The Pearl* to create a drama of the growth of conscious responsibility, but Kino's act of throwing away the pearl doesn't settle things for him as it did for the legendary fisherboy. The source offered a perfect tale of a man who consciously weighed the odds and chose hard work and poverty over being pestered all the time—a story that would have made a wonderfully tough-minded companion piece to *Cannery Row*.

Steinbeck, however, decided to give the legend some sentimental twists without realizing all the revisions that his first changes would necessitate. Perhaps such a basically fantastic, sentimental story does not warrant such strong condemnation; but *The Pearl* has been widely used as an introduction to fiction, and it provides the kind of introduction that is a disservice both to its author—who wrote much better, controlled works—and to fiction itself by failing to suggest the tough-minded complexity of the greatest examples of the art.

II   The Wayward Bus *(1947)*

The Wayward Bus does not warrant much critical attention, though we may wonder why Steinbeck himself expressed high hopes for this mechanical parable—for a parable this novel truly is, despite the fact that the applications of its morals are elusive. For his ambitious second parable of love, especially family love, Steinbeck made what would have seemed to be the wise choice of returning to the United States in the era during which he wrote. He chose a format that has been exploited with great success in novel and film from *Grand Hotel* and *Dinner at Eight* of the 1930s to such recent hits as *Airport* and *The Poseidon Adventure*. In these usually heavily melodramatic tales, a group of people, otherwise unrelated, are thrown together to face some common crisis in a public place or conveyance at a time when each of them is passing through some personal crisis. The format has been especially successful in elaborately produced films with all-star casts, but no truly profound work has ever employed it, probably because of the necessarily superficial characterization and jumpy construction of a work that moves back and forth between a number of diverse figures brought together arbitrarily.

As the vehicle for a journey fraught with perils, Steinbeck chooses a rickety old bus driven by Juan Chicoy (note those initials). The opening pages are heavy with symbolism. The bus travels between two main highways over a difficult back road from Rebel Corners to San Juan de la Cruz. The front bumper is a palimpsest on which the Spanish words for "the great power of Jesus" are still barely discernible beneath the new legend, "Sweetheart," which decorates both front and rear bumpers. The road from Rebel Corners leads at last, Steinbeck points out twice in four pages, to Hollywood, where, he adds snidely, "eventually, all the adolescents in the world will be congregated."

Those who gather at Juan Chicoy's crossroads store for the trip across the mountains one rainy day include Mr. Van Brunt (a cranky old man on the brink of death), Camille Oaks (a very sexy girl who performs a striptease act at businessmen's smokers), Ernest Horton (a former soldier who has won the Congressional Medal of Honor, but who must now earn a living by selling repulsive trick novelties), Mr. and Mrs. Pritchard (a prosperous businessman and his domineering wife), their daughter Mildred (a restless girl who would in a later decade have been a "Hippie"), Norma (a naïve, movie-struck waitress infatuated with Clark Gable), and "Pimples" Carson (an adolescent mechanic who consumes great quantities of cakes, candies, and pies, as sex substitutes). Juan Chicoy, the bus driver, Steinbeck introduces as "a fine, steady man." The only other important character is his shrewish wife Alice, an alcoholic, who stays at the store to get drunk when the bus departs.

Peter Lisca in *The Wide World of John Steinbeck* makes what has become a widely accepted division of these characters into three groups that he calls the damned, the saved, and those in purgatory.[5] While this division is plausible, it is of little assistance in relating *The Wayward Bus* to Steinbeck's other novels, for his interests are rarely narrowly theological. Most of his writings, beginning with *Cup of Gold*, display little respect for conventional Roman Catholic or Protestant theology; and the message of Jim Casy in *The Grapes of Wrath* may be summed up in the statement that each man must develop his own theology and work out his own salvation. Even though there are suggestions of a journey from hell to heaven in the names of Rebel Corners and San Juan de la Cruz, Steinbeck could have chosen these to create a social

rather than a theological allegory. At the very beginning of
the novel, he makes the point that the people for whom Rebel
Corners was named "have, through pride and a low threshold
of insult which is the test of ignorance and laziness, disappeared from the face of the earth"; and the particular selection
of Saint John of the Cross, author of *The Dark Night of the
Soul*, must be interpreted as an effort to find a figure who
symbolizes not just the institutions of the Christian religion
but the universal mystical tradition of the individual seeking
to transcend his senses. (Saint John of the Cross is more nearly
associated with Buddha, Plotinus, and Rumi than with most
other Christian leaders.) As in his earlier works, from *Cup
of Gold* to *The Grapes of Wrath*, Steinbeck is interested in
man's relationship to the society around him, not the afterlife.
(On the other hand, I find no grounds for reading the book
as "political" in the sense that it attacks or defends Capitalism,
Communism, or any other doctrine. While the passengers
briefly cooperate to get the bus back on the road when it is
mired, they never develop the sense of community that the
Joads do in *The Grapes of Wrath*; and, as the story ends, they
are preparing to go their separate ways.)

The characters in the novel can be grouped, I believe, most
satisfactorily—both in the light of the overall aim of this present
study and in the light of clarifying the novel's relationship
to Steinbeck's evolving philosophy of man—into what I have
been discussing throughout this study as Naturalistic and self-
conscious characters. *The Wayward Bus* is one of Steinbeck's
very few works in which the two types of characters are almost
equally emphasized and in which they come into open conflict
with each other.

Both kinds of characters do appear. The Naturalistic characters are Camille Oaks, Mr. Van Brunt, and Alice Chicoy, all
of whom find life full of "oaths and walking-sticks." Camille
is one of the "anomalies" that have so much intrigued Steinbeck, although she has rarely been mentioned in connection
with Tularecito, Lennie in *Of Mice and Men* and Frankie in
Cannery Row. Like them, she is a good-natured, well-meaning
person, who suffers from a physical handicap that she can
neither understand nor control. Although she is intelligent
enough to take care of herself (whereas most of the earlier
anomalies are not), she possesses, like Dreiser's Sister Carrie,

some kind of mysterious, irresistible sexual appeal to men. Van Brunt and Alice Chicoy, on the other hand, Steinbeck seems to suggest, simply indulge themselves and refuse to exercise any control over their behavior. Van Brunt knows that he is on the verge of a fatal stroke, but he can't bring himself to tell his wife or to end his life tidily by suicide. Instead he foolishly travels in bad weather on a risky public conveyance and throws temper tantrums that make his own condition worse and cause others discomfort. Alice Chicoy is aware of the consequences of drinking too much, but she can't stop drinking. (One of the most serious questions raised by the novel is Steinbeck's characterization of this group. Camille's mysterious appeal strains credibility, and many people are likely to look upon Van Brunt's temper and Alice's drinking as illnesses rather than self-indulgences.)

The characters who are fully in control of their behavior are Juan Chicoy, Ernest Horton, and Mr. and Mrs. Pritchard; but there is an important difference between Horton and Chicoy, on the one hand, and the Pritchards, on the other. The former pair of men are true to themselves, regardless of what others may think of them; the Pritchards, however, have consciously adopted masks to conceal their true selves and to make themselves more socially attractive. Mr. Pritchard is a latter-day Henry Morgan, who has "split up" before the demands of civilization: "Wherever he went he was not one man but a unit in a corporation, a unit in a club, in a lodge, in a church, in a political party. His thoughts and ideas were never subjected to criticism since he *willingly* associated only with people like himself. . . . He did not want to stand out from his group" (italics mine). His wife is less "split up" than devious. "Having few actual perceptions," Steinbeck observes, "she lived by rules"; but she keeps these rules to herself and exercises power over her husband, her daughter, and other people around her by suffering frequent "headaches" and using her indisposition to manipulate her family and friends.

As a result of the difference between Chicoy and Horton's blunt honesty and the Pritchards' hypocrisy, Steinbeck seems to suggest, the former two men are punished by being relegated to menial, even degrading work that fails to utilize their talents; whereas the Pritchards are rewarded with wealth and powerful positions despite their comparatively mediocre talents.

Steinbeck confronts these Naturalistic and two kinds of self-conscious characters with each other in *The Wayward Bus* in order to study the problem that surely most concerned him after World War II—the respective influences that these groups might have on determining the not yet fully formed characters of the three young people in the novel, Mildred Pritchard, Norma the waitress, and Pimples Carson. Though much older than Jody Tiflin in *The Red Pony*, all three young people stand —as Jody did—on the verge of psychological maturity. All three seem, furthermore, to be teetering on the brink of a disastrous self-indulgence that will doom them to the fates of Van Brunt and Alice Chicoy. Mildred Pritchard's casual promiscuity and young Carson's unquenchable appetite for sweets are evidences of gross, sensual self-indulgence; and Norma's unrequited love for movie stars portends a disastrous detachment from reality even more pathetic than Camille Oaks's forced withdrawal from society to avoid unwanted attentions.

If the three young people are to gain conscious control of themselves they must be inspired by a powerful model whose appeal will prove stronger than animal appetites or aimless dreaming. Mr. and Mrs. Pritchard would like to provide such a model with their money and their social position, but the three young people are repulsed by the Pritchards' hypocrisy, haughtiness, and bigotry. The example must come from Ernest Horton or Juan Chicoy if it is to be provided at all. The real dramatic tension in the novel, therefore, is provided by both men's very nearly compromising their integrity out of disgust with their situations. Ashamed of his job, Horton contemplates a business deal with Pritchard that would enrich him at the expense of his prized individuality. Disgusted with his responsibilities and his wife's alcoholism, Juan Chicoy thinks about just heading for the hills like "a ferryboat captain in New York who just headed out to sea one day and they never heard from him again." When during the trip across the mountain, the bus becomes mired in the mud, Juan does abandon it and his passengers.

The author's philosophy will be reflected by Horton's and Juan's final decisions: if Horton compromises and Juan runs away, the irresponsible and hypocritical characters will triumph and the book will be another Naturalistic tragedy like

Of Mice and Men. On the other hand, if Horton retains his integrity and Juan returns to his duties, *The Wayward Bus* will be a high comedy of consciousness triumphant. Horton does refuse to compromise; and, after fornicating with Mildred Pritchard, Juan does return to his duties. The bus moves on towards the lights of San Juan de la Cruz. Steinbeck even underscores his concept of the way that things ought to turn out by having the Pritchards' hypocritical masks stripped away when—during the time that the bus is mired—Mr. Pritchard brushes aside his wife's pleas of "headache" and virtually rapes her. The young people are apparently salvaged. Norma has succeeded in her effort to break free from Alice Chicoy's oppressive dominance, and she talks realistically with Camille about sharing an apartment in Los Angeles. After her affair with Juan, the formerly petulant Mildred Pritchard becomes cheerful and cooperative. Young Carson gains self-assurance when Juan begins to call him "Kit" instead of "Pimples" and gives him responsibility for the passengers.

In the blueprint just set forth, *The Wayward Bus* gives every promise of being a sound, complex, exciting, affirmative work; and Steinbeck wrote enthusiastically to his publishers that he had high hopes for the book. The plotting is somewhat mechanical, but Steinbeck had earlier used such obvious constructions in some of his most successful works like *The Red Pony* and *In Dubious Battle*, even *The Grapes of Wrath*. The novel was, however, poorly received by contemporary reviewers and has since been almost unanimously attacked by critics. Particularly in view of Steinbeck's preoccupation in the characterization of Juan Chicoy with the image of "the good mechanic," what went wrong with Steinbeck's own mechanism?

The first of the two principal shortcomings of the work is that readers are *told* too much and not *shown* enough. In summarizing earlier the success of *The Red Pony*, I observed that the morals of this story-cycle are not so obvious as my explanation makes them seem. In *The Wayward Bus*, however, the messages are more obvious than an outline of the book suggests. Steinbeck spends too much time in this book talking *about* his characters rather than *through* them. Lester Jay Marks best sums up the problem in *Thematic Design in the Novels of John Steinbeck:* "Even the allegorical novel, if it is to be successful as a novel, must create a convincing plot and convincing characters, so that the reader may be led, by indirection, to its allegorical meaning. In *The Wayward Bus* Steinbeck overtly tells his meanings; his characters are explained more than they are described, and action is subordinated to such explanation."[6] The result is a sluggish tale that is one-quarter over before Juan's yearning to "just head for the hills" is disclosed and half over before the bus ride ever begins.

Steinbeck's failure in telling rather than showing is particularly striking in his characterization of Juan Chicoy. In a letter to his editor Steinbeck explained that Juan was supposed to be "all the god the fathers you ever saw driving a six cylinder broken down battered world through time and space."[7] The success of the book depended more than anything else upon Steinbeck's making readers see Juan that way, and unfortunately he doesn't. Joseph Fontenrose has summed up the general reaction to the character: "... Juan is hardly a convincing character. His streak of cruelty seems more believable than his superior objectivity.... But his transcendent role obscures these credible touches of earthiness. We have a Realistic story told as a morality of Everyman; but though the narrative skill displayed is great, vehicle and tenor do not jibe."[8]

The second major shortcoming of the work also illustrates Fontenrose's objection to the incompatibility of vehicle and tenor, because the three most striking passages in the novel are virtuoso accounts of Camille Oaks's effect upon a Greyhound bus driver (not Juan Chicoy), Alice Chicoy's getting drunk, and Van Brunt's fatal stroke. Yet these brilliantly executed passages seem digressions because they focus attention upon Naturalistic characters, whose situations are already fixed and irremediable, at the expense of the development of Juan Chicoy and Ernest Horton, who—as the previous analysis of the structuring of the novel indicates—are the intended protagonists and who should make the most powerful impact upon both the impressionable young characters in the novel and its readers. A comparable dramatic effect could have been obtained in *The Grapes of Wrath*, for example, by having Uncle John's behavior as a result of his guilt feelings overshadow the killing of Casy; as Fontenrose protests, tenor and vehicle do not jibe. While Steinbeck was determined to make the conscious representatives of integrity and responsibility come out winners, he presented more vividly the Naturalistic victims of uncontrollable forces who resembled the characters he had written about during the 1930s. (*East of Eden* was to suffer from the same lack of reconciliation between theory and practice.)

The Wayward Bus thus patches together but never really fuses a heartening parable about a kind of folk superman—who consciously surrenders his own self-indulgent desires to escape to a life of ease in order to carry out his duty of delivering his passengers to their destinations—with a brilliant and sardonic novel about a decaying world of Naturalistic types. These types are the "Atomites," as Steinbeck calls them at one point, "who, for some unknown reason, disappeared from the face of the earth." In his next play-novelette, Steinbeck attempted to drop the Naturalistic material altogether; and he succeeded in creating a work that is a pure, self-contained parable. Unfortunately, *Burning Bright* is also the dullest book that he wrote. Steinbeck was searching his imagination for new heroes to rise from among the people and lead them, but he didn't seem to be able to come up with any.

III   Viva Zapata!

Actually, Steinbeck's most successful production during this period was his fictionalized history of a genuine folk hero, Emiliano Zapata, for Elia Kazan's film *Viva Zapata!*, which starred Marlon Brando as the Mexican rebel leader. Unfortunately, dependable access to the finished film is difficult; but the script is being published. As Robert Morsberger describes the work, however, it treats Zapata not as a revolutionary, but as an example of what Albert Camus defines as a rebel: a man willing to die for freedom rather than one who speaks of liberty but establishes terror. Offered power during the Mexican civil wars early in the twentieth century, Zapata mysteriously disappeared. Although conflicting stories exist about his motives for vanishing, Steinbeck and Kazan chose to interpret Zapata's behavior as a conscious renunciation of

power once he had realized the way it would compromise
his integrity—a decision that ultimately led to his death at
the hands of those who could no longer manipulate him.[9]
Zapata behaves in the film in much the same way that Kino
does in *The Pearl* and that Ernest Horton does in *The Wayward
Bus*. Steinbeck was much less successful in these novels, however, when he tried to create a folk figure who became a hero
by consciously making selfless choices, than he was when
he worked from history in collaboration with another powerful
artist, Elia Kazan, to create *Viva Zapata!*

The collaboration, of course, makes it impossible to compare
this work precisely with the novels that were exclusively Steinbeck's invention, especially since in any effective film drama
it is the director who finally shapes the characters. Despite
the difficulty in singling out Steinbeck's contributions to the
film, however, Morsberger's enthusiastic conclusion that "far
from being a digression into Hollywood," *Viva Zapata!* "sums
up issues that had long been central" to Steinbeck's work
is valid and indicates that the script cannot be ignored in tracing
the development of Steinbeck's philosophy of man. But Morsberger's enthusiasm needs, too, to be tempered by the re-
membrance that Steinbeck had earlier created a Camusian
rebel in his portrayal of Casy in *The Grapes of Wrath*.

IV   Burning Bright

Burning Bright attempts to reverse the situation in *Viva
Zapata!* by disposing of the villain and letting the humble
hero survive. Joe Saul, a middle-aged man, is married for the
second time to a girl named Mordeen. He has never had any
children, and his new wife suspects that childhood rheumatic
fever rendered him sterile. Although the couple's closest
friend, Ed, refuses to encourage her, Mordeen decides to try
to have a child by Victor, a strong, brash young man who
does not belong to Joe Saul's tradition. When Mordeen
becomes pregnant, Victor becomes upset at being used and
wants her to run away with him; but Ed swings into action
and eliminates Victor. Joe Saul has discovered, however, that
he is sterile and comes home outraged. At last, however, he
recognizes, "I thought my blood must survive—my line—but

it's not so. . . . It is the race, the species that must go staggering on. . . . I love the child . . . I love our child . . . *I love my son.*"

While the idea that everyone is responsible for all the world's children can hardly be faulted as a theme for a UNICEF fund drive, such unrelieved moralizing hardly provides a stimulating theatergoing experience. Whether to universalize the message or to attempt to increase the appeal of the work, Steinbeck decided to use some unimpressive and confusing gimmicks in unfolding his parable. In the first act, the characters are circus performers; in the second, farmers; in the third, seamen, although they continue to bear the same relationships to one another as husband, wife, lover, friend. Also the second act begins in June and ends at Christmas, although the action is continuous. Steinbeck apparently supposed that such devices would suggest the relationship of his present-day work to the tradition of early morality plays like *Everyman.* He attempts to prepare the audience for the shifts to come in later acts by having Joe Saul say in the first one, "I know it is a thing that can happen to anyone, in any place or time—a farmer or a sailor, of a lifeless, faceless Everyone!"

The words *lifeless* and *faceless* are singularly unfortunate choices in this context, and the use of all these devices only succeeded in confusing theatergoers, some of whom supposed that circus performers must spend part of the year on a farm. The reader has the uneasy feeling that the action literally takes to sea in the last act so that Victor can be pushed overboard; his abrupt disappearance would be less easily managed elsewhere. Even Steinbeck himself finally admitted to Peter Lisca that the work was "too abstract" and "preached too much" and—most fatal to the success of drama—"the audience was always a step ahead of it."[10]

Nothing is accomplished by an extensive post mortem. The work is remembered today only because of its relationship to Steinbeck's efforts to create a convincing drama of consciousness. It suggests the perhaps insuperable difficulties of creating a self-conscious folk hero; and, unfortunately, Steinbeck persisted in the effort to devise such a hero in *East of Eden,* his next major project and his most ambitious novel, in which he turned what might have been a nostalgic idyll of a passing pastoral age into what is most often recalled as another implausible dramatization of the discovery of an affirmative philosophy.

CHAPTER 10

East of Eden—
California and the Cosmic California

"COULDN'T a world be built around accepted truths? Couldn't some pains and insanities be rooted out if the the causes were known?" gently asks a Chinese character identified only as Lee as *East of Eden* (1952) lumbers towards its intellectual/philosophical climax (271).[1] The "examined life" that the drama of consciousness portrays should result in exactly the kind of world that Lee pleads for, and in this big novel Steinbeck tries to portray the difficult attainment of such a fully conscious, examined life. He attempts to dramatize a plan for remaking the world.

Such a model for the evolution of the world is called a *cosmogony*. Thornton Wilder illustrates most clearly the meaning of the term in his description in *The Eighth Day* of the Kangaheela Indians' "Book of Promises"—"to boys and girls it made clear why they were born and why the universe was set in motion." In the more thunderous rhetoric of a classic work to which Steinbeck often referred, John Milton's *Paradise Lost*, a cosmogony is a sacred text that seeks "to justify the ways of God to man."

Actually nearly all of Steinbeck's fictions beginning with *The Grapes of Wrath* exemplify the parable form of most sacred writings, but his principal claim to the title of *cosmogonist* is his ambitious history of a modern American Adam. Indeed, the major character in *East of Eden* is even named Adam. Further evidence that Steinbeck is quite consciously writing about the evolution of a heightened consciousness is evident from entries in the posthumously published *Journal of a Novel: The "East of Eden" Letters,* which contains daily reports addressed during the composition of the novel to Steinbeck's long-time editor and friend Pascal Covici, but not delivered until after the novel was completed. The reports provide a unique account of the writer's feelings, aims, and achievements

141

as he was working on what he regarded as his "big novel."
The story was not just about the Trask family, Steinbeck wrote
an April 23, 1951, two months after starting work; it was "about
the whole Salinas Valley which I am using as a microcosm
of the whole nation." "Consciousness" was much on the
author's mind as he wrote, for this entry continues, "I think
I know better what I am doing than most writers," although
he self-effacingly adds, "But it still isn't much" (65).[2] "These
people are essentially symbol people," he comments on March
12 (27).

The artistic merits or shortcomings of *East of Eden* have
been the subject of a long and rancorous debate that need
not be summarized here; but the general—and seemingly inescapable—conclusion is that, as fiction, the novel is only sporad-
ically interesting because the "symbol people" never come
to life for readers, as repeated entries in his journal suggest
that they did for Steinbeck. But, whatever the artistic merits,
East of Eden is a work that the author took very seriously;
moreover, this novel is crucially important to illustrating the
distinction between Naturalistic fiction and the drama of consciousness because of the author's preoccupation with the
problems of man's conscious responsibilities for his actions.

A central concern that eventually nearly overshadows all
others in the long, complex novel is the interpretation of a
Hebrew verb in Genesis IV, 7. According to the King James
version of the Bible, God says to Cain, "And if thou doest
not well, sin lieth at the door. And unto thee shall be his
desire, and *thou shalt rule over him*" (italics mine). The passage bothers the character Lee, the bookish Chinese house-
man; and, when he finds in the American Standard Bible the
italicized words translated "Do thou rule over him," he per-
suades four ancient Chinese scholars to learn Hebrew in order
to find the proper reading of the passage. After two years,
they arrive at the conclusion that it should read, "Thou mayest
rule over sin." Lee excitedly explains the importance of this
discovery:

"The American Standard translation *orders* men to triumph over sin,
and you can call sin ignorance. The King James translation makes
a promise in 'Thou Shalt,' meaning that men will surely triumph
over sin. But the Hebrew word, the word *timshel*—'Thou mayest'

—that gives a choice. It might be the most important word in the world. That says the way is open. That throws it right back on a man. For if 'Thou mayest'—it is also true that 'Thou mayest not' " (303).

Doubts have been expressed about Steinbeck's interpretation of *timshel*; but, since no one turns to American novelists for accurate Hebrew scholarship, the important thing is that Steinbeck constructs his fiction around the theory that *timshel* should be translated *thou mayest*. What matters is not what Steinbeck tells us about the Bible, but what he tells us about his own philosophy through his use of the Bible. Therefore, *East of Eden* does not necessarily give us God's concept of man's destiny; it gives us John Steinbeck's. Steinbeck is constructing a cosmogony as surely as William Blake did.

Very probably, however, Steinbeck uses symbolism from the Judaeo-Christian Bible rather than from a privately conceived mythology like Blake's to explain matters to readers in terms that they would find familiar and comprehensible, and to avoid the obscurities of works like Blake's prophetic poems. Use of the Bible does not necessarily mean, however, literal belief in it; and arguments against a novel on the basis of the author's misconstruction of biblical texts misconstrue the nature of fiction. If we wish to assail Steinbeck's inferences, doing that is quite another matter. We may still, however, have misgivings about the vitality of fiction in which character development is subordinated to theological speculation and cosmogony building. Yet heavy-handed as Steinbeck's speculation becomes in *East of Eden*, it is not simply imposed upon the story—as the message is in the final scene of *Burning Bright*. In *East of Eden*, the theories discussed are dramatized in those episodes that lead up to the major climax.

Up to the point of Lee's revelations, *East of Eden* meanders back and forth between two narratives—one is based on Steinbeck's mother's family, the Hamiltons, who are called by their proper names; the other is based on the lurid history of the fictional family of Adam Trask. Samuel Hamilton, Steinbeck's maternal grandfather, is presented as a kind of fisher-king, as a benign wizard who can locate hidden water on everyone's property but his own and who can make money through his water-witching and inventions that others exploit for everyone but himself and his nine children. Adam Trask is the son of a Connecticut farmer who apparently embezzled a small fortune while a promoter for the Grand Army of the Republic (the organization of Union veterans of the Civil War). Adam is bedazzled into marrying Cathy (later Kate) Ames, an embodiment of evil, who—among other things—has burned her parents to death in their home and has been in turn nearly beaten to death by a pimp that she has been cheating.

Arriving in California, Cathy bears twin sons (later named Aron and Caleb) that Samuel Hamilton helps deliver; then she seriously wounds Adam in order to escape his house and establish herself in nearby Salinas as the mistress of an extraordinary bordello, a backwoods version of the decadent setting of Jean Genet's play *The Balcony*; and, in the process of taking it over, Kate poisons the former owner. After being abandoned, Adam succumbs to melancholia and doesn't even get around for years to naming the twins, who are cared for by the ever-resourceful Lee.

Just about everybody in the neighborhood except Adam and the twins knows that his wife is alive and what she is doing; but no one has the temerity to enlighten the bereaved husband until Sam Hamilton—fortified by Lee's recital of the *timshel* investigation—takes the responsibility of telling him. As Sam explains his action afterward to Lee,

"I do not believe all men are destroyed.... Surely most men are destroyed, but there are others who like pillars of fire guide frightened men through the darkness. 'Thou mayest, Thou mayest!' What glory!... the choice, Lee the choice of winning! I had never understood it or accepted it before. Do you see now why I told Adam tonight? I exercised the choice. Maybe I was wrong, but by telling him I also forced him to live or get off the pot." (308–09)

The choice proves wise. Adam visits Cathy's establishment, and the talismanic word that Lee and Samuel have provided him exorcises her spell over him and returns him to life. Ironically, Samuel once again wins for everyone but himself: he dies as Adam begins to live again.

After Samuel's death, his family falls to pieces. "When Samuel Hamilton died," Lee observes mournfully as the book nears its end, "the world went out like a candle. I relighted it to see his lovely creations, and I saw his children tossed and torn and destroyed as though some vengefulness was at work" (600). But the failure of Samuel's progeny only briefly depresses Lee. He attributes to his own "stupidity" his conclusion that "the good are destroyed while the evil survive and prosper," because he argues that "every man in every generation is refired. . . . All impurities burned out and ready for a glorious flux, and for that—more fire. And then either the slag heap, or, perhaps what no one in world ever quite gives up, perfection" (600). The implication of the second climax of the novel is, therefore, that Samuel Hamilton's good work may at last triumph through the long-suffering Trasks.

When Cathy's baneful spell is lifted, Adam sufficiently recovers his spirits to buy a Ford; to go back into business in Salinas where the growing twins are almost certain to hear about, perhaps even meet, the mother that they have been told is dead; and then to lose most of his money in a visionary scheme to send refrigerated lettuce across country to eastern markets. Attracted to the ministry, twin Aron becomes increasingly saintly; but the dark brother Caleb, spurred by the discovery of the truth about his mother, begins to fancy himself evil. He proves, however, impervious to her witchery. Confronting her, he asks, "When you were little, did you . . . ever have the feeling that you were missing something? Like as if the others knew something you didn't—like a secret they wouldn't tell you?" This woman, who has committed murder without batting an eyelash, panics at these probings and begins to withdraw into herself; but Caleb revels in the knowledge that he does not have *her* evil in him, "It just came to me whole. If I'm mean, it's my own mean" (465–66).

Caleb shields Aron from knowledge that their mother is alive until father Adam refuses to accept as a gift to restore his fortune a large sum that Cal has earned through wartime speculation (World War I has arrived on the scene) in beans. (Kate had, incidentally, earlier killed her patroness with poisoned beans.) Despite Lee's pleas that Cal control himself, "You have a choice" (Lee does not use the word *timshel*, but by this time the reader can supply it as Lennie in *Of Mice and Men* could the final words of George's chant), the disgruntled Cal takes his innocent brother to what is known as Kate's "circus," where perverted acts are performed for money. Aron cannot bear the sight of such evil and runs away

to join the army. Defeated by Cal and finding her past beginning to catch up with her, Kate commits suicide. Aron is killed
in battle; Adam suffers what will surely prove a fatal stroke,
Cal, left alone, is overwhelmed by guilt.

Lee, however, forces his way and Cal's to Adam's deathbed;
and there, for the exorcistic denouement of the book, he pleads
that Caleb "did a thing in anger, Adam, because he thought
you had rejected him." Although the other watchers are hor-
rified when Lee puts the screws to a dying man, the determined
Chinese continues: " 'I have to. . . . If it kills him I have to.
I have the choice," and he smiled sadly and quoted, "If there's
blame, it's my blame. . . . Adam, give him your blessing. Don't
leave him alone with his guilt' " (602). Adam forces his lips
to utter the word, *"Timshel!"*

This parable of the exorcism of destructive, irrational
impulses by choosing to exercise the power man possesses
to control consciously his behavior does not succeed so neatly
in the novel, however, as in this summary because Steinbeck
seems unable to exercise the full, conscious control necessary
over the shaping of the symbols essential to the success of
the undertaking. The basic problem—as many readers have
perceived—is the character of Cathy/Kate, whom Steinbeck
introduces in this way:

> I believe there are monsters born in this world to human parents.
> Some you can see, misshapen and horrible. . . . Once they were consi-
> dered the visible punishments for concealed sins.
> And just as there are physical monsters, can there not be mental
> or psychic monsters born . . .?
> It is my belief that Cathy Ames was born with the tendencies,
> or lack of them, which drove and forced her all her life. . . . There
> was a time when a girl like Cathy would have been called possessed
> by the devil. . . . She would have been burned as a witch for the
> good of the community (72–73).

However we may choose to interpret the term *witch*, Cathy
certainly is one. If an author is, however, to structure his argument on the basis of the Hebraic book of Genesis—as Steinbeck
does in using his interpretation of *timshel* as the key to man's
potential for conscious control over his impulses—he has to
be consistent, for purposes of argument, with his source. There
were devils and witches in biblical days, like the snakes to

which Kate is often metaphorically compared, especially when she bites Sam Hamilton (195). In terms of the symbolic framework that Steinbeck borrows, Kate is a witch whose spell must be exorcised if her activities are not to continue to destroy innocent people. But Steinbeck's attitude was probably too "scientific" to allow him to deal matter of factly with witchcraft (he would overcome this reluctance by the time he wrote his last novel, *The Winter of Our Discontent*). In the literal-minded Eisenhower years, Steinbeck may well have been concerned about what people would say if he started talking seriously about witches. Thus we find later in the novel:

> When I said Cathy was a monster it seemed to me that it was so. Now I have bent close with a glass over the small print of her and reread the footnotes, and I wonder if it is true. The trouble is that since we cannot know what she wanted, we will never know whether or not she got it. . . . Her life may have been her language, formal, developed, indecipherable. It is easy to say she was bad, but there is little meaning unless we know why (184).

The trouble with this shift of ground is that Steinbeck is not writing the biography of a real person. He created Cathy; and, in the very terms of the *timshel* argument in the novel, he is responsible for his creations. There can be no "footnotes" to sources outside himself. As Wayne Booth maintains in *The Rhetoric of Fiction*, "the author's judgment is always present . . . though the author can to some extent choose his disguises, he can never choose to disappear."[3] But Steinbeck does try to disappear from *East of Eden*, possibly in order to create the kind of "open-ended" parable of which Lawrence William Jones speaks, one which each reader must interpret for himself. However, an author cannot offer us a hypothetical figure of his own creation and then start puzzling over its interpretation. If we find his initial hypothesis dubious (as many readers have), we still may accept it for the sake of argument if he maintains it consistently; but, if he himself doesn't want to take responsibility for what he's doing, the whole effort is a waste of everyone's time.

In *Journal of a Novel*, Steinbeck, foreseeing objections to his new novel, rails against what he calls "expecters": "It will not be what anyone expects and so the expecters will not like it. And until it gets to people who don't expect anything

and are just willing to go along with the story, no one is likely
to like this book" (26). But it is too much to ask readers to
"go along" with a story when they're not sure whether the
author is thinking of his characters as laboratory specimens
or as real folks.

Kate is not the only character that Steinbeck fails to manage
consistently. Describing her twin sons when they are young,
the author writes:

> Maybe the difference between the two boys can best be described
> in this way. If Aron should come upon an anthill in a little clearing
> in the brush, he would lie on his stomach and watch the complications
> of ant life. . . . If, on the other hand, Cal came upon the same anthill,
> he would kick it to pieces and watch while the frantic ants took
> care of their disaster. Aron was content to be a part of his world,
> but Cal must change it (348–49).

Steinbeck makes a great deal of this contrast in explaining
Cal's early behavior; but we later learn that Aron reacted as
he did to the discovery of the truth about his mother because
"that's not how he wanted the story to go—and he wouldn't
have any other story, so he tore up the world" (578). Early
in the novel, Lee tells Sam Hamilton, "You are one of those
rare people who can separate your observation from your pre-
conception" (163); and the first description quoted above of
Aron makes him sound like this type of person; but the second
one makes it seem that Cal (who is speaking) is this type
and that Aron isn't.

Of course people change, but Steinbeck never prepares for
any change in the twins as they grow. In dealing with both
Cathy and Aron, Steinbeck does not seem to have gone back
in order to bring his early descriptions in line with later
developments, as he could very easily have done, for example,
by simply theorizing at the beginning of the book that there
might be psychic monsters instead of flatly asserting that there
are. The descriptions of Cathy are not the opinions of characters
who may change their minds in the course of events; they
are the work of an author who is responsible for controlling
his work so that the parts finally harmonize with each other.
As a result of these discords in the author's viewpoint, it is
not possible to read *East of Eden* on several levels as Steinbeck
maintained we could read *The Grapes of Wrath* and *Cannery*

Row. It is impossible to present any consistent allegory through a story that is confused on the literal level.

Steinbeck's attitude toward the novel has been clarified by the publication of *Journal of a Novel,* in which he often talks about his characters as though they were real people that he was trying to understand rather than symbols that he had created. "Why Adam Trask should have fallen in love with [Cathy] is anybody's guess," he writes on March 27; "but I think it was because he himself was trained to operate best under a harsh master and simply transferred that to a tough mistress" (39). This technique is a dubious fictional one, for the reason for the behavior of fictional characters should not be "anybody's guess," since they are not "anybody's" characters but the author's. The novelist seems to have fallen into the common trap of confusing his private opinion with universal truth; but doing so is, of course, a mark of the cosmogonist. In the preface to *Cannery Row,* Steinbeck had the modesty to observe that each man saw the place through his own "peephole" and that one man found "whores" and "pimps" where another found "saints and angels." By the time he wrote *East of Eden,* Steinbeck seems to have developed the arrogant notion that he had achieved a detachment that transcends such biased visions, so that he need simply create a cosmos for others to interpret.

Also in *Cannery Row,* Steinbeck spoke of "the hurried mangled craziness of Monterey and the cosmic Monterey," but he gave us only Monterey and let us imagine the cosmos. In *East of Eden,* he insists on providing both rather than on presenting one and leaving the reader to discover the other through exercising his imagination. Such a failing is, perhaps, inevitable in any novel in which an author chooses to use members of his own family—bearing their own names—as characters. The decision to introduce the Hamiltons into a novel was unfortunate for two reasons, neither of which is that the things reported of them might not be "true," as Steinbeck asserts in *Journal of a Novel* that they are. The first reason is that while the author may (and *only* may) know the facts about his family, he may not understand them even so well as an outsider might. He can, therefore, in a biography, legitimately pose questions of the kind that he does about Cathy's motivation; but in a novel he must take responsibility for what he has created.

The second reason is that it is hard to believe that even the most gifted author could give readers the sense of involvement that he himself feels about characters based directly on his family. Steinbeck argues in *Journal of a Novel* that "the great story of the Hamiltons is that of Uncle Tom and his sister Dessie and of the death of Dessie and Tom's suicide" (69). Readers are likely to feel that the handling of this "great story" in the novel (389–410) means more to the author than to them because the motives for the characters' behavior are not clear, and it is difficult for the reader who does not know them as people to feel concern about them unless he can develop the sense that these characters are of special significance for some reason besides being related to the novelist.

Readers sometimes wonder why Thomas Wolfe made such a change as that of the name of his fictional alter ego first to Eugene Gant and then to George Webber, or that of Asheville, North Carolina, to Altamont, Catawba. I think that we can see the wisdom of Wolfe's practice from Steinbeck's failure to use it. Eugene Gant is not Thomas Wolfe, and Asheville is not Altamont; for closely as they in some ways resemble things in the real world, they exist only in the mind of Thomas Wolfe. They are fantasies that offer commentaries on the realities that they mimic. In *East of Eden*, biography (which may be a pack of lies, but which is offered as a mirror of reality and not as an invention) and fiction cannot be distinguished; and the result is that the very "conscious control" needed to provide a philosophical framework for the action is missing. Such a lack would be disastrous to the artistic consistency of any work; but it is especially devastating to the success of a cosmogony in which the author attempts to make clear to boys and girls why the universe was set in motion. The success of such a work depends upon a clear, consistent vision that is not distracted from its labor of creating a harmonious universe by the perverse developments sometimes encountered in real life.

John McAleer argues in "*An American Tragedy* and *In Cold Blood*" that Dreiser's novel has a social urgency that Capote's "non-fiction novel" lacks because Capote becomes bogged down in petty facts while Dreiser's fictionalizing his material liberated him from details so that he might make his story an attack upon the consequences of the American dream.[4]

McAleer's argument applies to *East of Eden* as it contrasts to *Look Homeward, Angel* because Steinbeck also was concerned in this major work with the consequences of the American dream. Near the end of the novel, Lee holds forth to Cal on Americans as violent people:

"If our ancestors had not been that, they would have stayed in their home plots in the other world and starved over the squeezed-out soil. . . . All colors and blends of Americans have somewhat the same tendencies. It's a breed—selected out by accident. . . . In the old lands they say of us that we go from barbarism to decadence without an intervening culture. Can it be that our critics have not the key or the language of our culture?" (570).

The finding of a "key" to our language and culture, however, is again the business of the biographer, not the novelist—especially since, if the "American breed" has been selected out "by accident," it affords no support for the *timshel* doctrine propounded by the characters in the book. Philosophically, *East of Eden* is a parable, like *Burning Bright*, that dramatizes how people *should* behave; but the Hamilton family chapters are accounts of the often mysterious ways that people *did* behave.

Sometimes we find ourselves in a place where a television set disconcertingly picks up the picture from one station and the sound from another. The writing of *East of Eden* seems to have found Steinbeck in just such a spot. The warm, personal beauty of the Hamilton story looks forward to the affectionate reports of American life in *Travels with Charley* and in *America and Americans*; but the Trask family story shows that the author was not content to describe life and let the readers draw their own conclusions but had to moralize through a parable involving characters in which it is difficult to believe. Steinbeck argued in an abandoned preface to *East of Eden* that was subsequently printed in *Journal of a Novel* that he had not "written two books and stuck them together," but that instead he had "written about one family and used stories about another family as well as counterpoint, as rest, as contrast in pace and color" (180). Rather than counterpointing each other, however, the two stories clash, because the characters in the Hamilton story are believable, sympathetic, familiar, even if not so interesting to the reader as to Steinbeck himself, but the characters in the Trask story are incredible and thoroughly nasty and priggish, though fascinating to readers with prurient tastes. A writer can counterpoint Naturalistic and self-conscious characters, as Steinbeck does, for example, in *The Wayward Bus*, in which the two kinds offer alternative models for the still incompletely formed young people in the story; but, although *The Wayward Bus* is an artificial and unconvincing book for reasons already discussed in chapter 9, at least the two groups of characters share enough similarities to communicate with each other and intermingle freely. In *East of Eden*, just about the only overlapping of the Hamilton and Trask stories occurs when Samuel Hamilton visits Adam Trask or Lee; and we get from these scenes the same feeling that we do from those scenes in some of Walt Disney's motion pictures of the 1940s, like *Saludos Amigos!* in which live actors and cartoon characters sang and danced together. The trickery is impressive, but it doesn't have much relationship to life. In *East of Eden*, as in *The Wayward Bus*, the trouble is simply that Steinbeck's Naturalistic characters are better drawn and more convincing than his self-conscious characters. The difference between the writer's success in handling the two types of characters would not be so noticeable or objectionable if the more successfully drawn characters were ultimately the more important; but in *East of Eden*, the more poorly handled characters bear the burden of projecting the important "message" of the novel. The Hamiltons strike us as being present in the book only to remind us how well Steinbeck could write when he wasn't preoccupied with some heavy-handed allegory. Instead of counterpointing each other harmoniously, the two stories clash and confuse the reader just as a television picture with the wrong sound does, so that we are finally left with the discomforting feeling that, intently as Steinbeck sought after World War II to write dramas of consciousness, he remained essentially a Naturalistic writer who was more successful in portraying sympathetically the confused and defeated than in dramatizing intellectual solutions to man's dilemmas.

CHAPTER 11

Beyond the Drama of Consciousness

THE materials that Steinbeck selected for his earliest
published novels show that he did not feel at that
point in his career that *love*—in the particular sense of human
affection—was an adequate counterforce to the natural obstacles with which man must contend. Henry Morgan in *Cup
of Gold* gives up what he considers "love" (at least infatuation)
for financial security, and the fiction from *To a God Unknown*
to *Of Mice and Men* presents the view that the forces of violence and death are stronger than the power of love.

The Grapes of Wrath, however, presents a newfound conviction that love, informed by a developing consciousness,
may prevail in a hostile world. Then, in the works from *The
Grapes of Wrath* to *The Pearl*, Steinbeck equates the development of consciousness with the development of conscience.
(Hence the emphasis on Jim's Casy's echo of Christ's cry,
"Father, forgive them for they know not what they do," and
the implication is that, if they did know what they were doing,
they would be motivated by the promise of love that Christ
symbolized and would behave differently.) In *The Pearl*, all
the characters except Kino's wife are afflicted with an irrational
lust for material wealth. When Kino at last develops the consciousness that allows him to forsake his materialistic dream,
he simultaneously develops the conscience that allows him
to throw back into the sea the great pearl that so excites the
evil forces in men's natures. A basic objection to *The Pearl*,
especially as an introduction to serious literature, is the naïveté
of a view that equates the development of man's heart and
spirit with the development of his mind.

As early as *The Wayward Bus*, but most especially in *Burning
Bright* and *East of Eden*, Steinbeck demonstrated that he recognized that a man capable of consciously examining his
motives might not develop a compassionate conscience. Mr.
Pritchard in *The Wayward Bus* uses his consciousness to hide
his individual feelings, in order to improve his social and finan-

cial position. Mordeen stresses throughout *Burning Bright* that the quality that Victor fatally lacks, despite his intelligence, is affection; and Cathy/Kate Trask in *East of Eden* is Steinbeck's ultimate embodiment of the individual who is doubly separated from the people around her by her possession of a heightened consciousness and by her total lack of conscience.

The trouble with these three novels—as we have already seen in the two preceding chapters—is that the characters seem invented simply for the sake of the message. Although Steinbeck proposed Juan Chicoy, Joe Saul, and Adam Trask as antitheses to Mr. Pritchard, Victor, and Kate, he did not succeed in making their portrayals as men who use their consciousnesses to develop a conscientious sense of responsibility for others convincing enough to make the message seem to grow out of the character. Consequently, the three stories never become more than two-dimensional morality plays.

Steinbeck had not, in short, succeeded by the time that he completed his most ambitious novel, *East of Eden*, in creating a self-conscious character with a compassionate conscience who would display not just the passive goodwill towards all men that characterizes Doc in *Cannery Row*, but who could also serve as a dynamic force in remaking the world. Such an accomplishment may be too much to expect of any author. But whether the fault lies in Steinbeck's misassessment of his own capacities or in the failure of the world he observed to provide an appropriately heroic model, he never again achieved the fusion of story and philosophy, vehicle and tenor, that he had in *Cannery Row*. He did strive, however, in three final novels—*Sweet Thursday, The Short Reign of Pippin IV*, and *The Winter of Our Discontent*—to create characters who were both smart enough and affectionate enough to try to play an active role in making the world around them a better place. These efforts were not very successful; even the best of the three novels, *The Short Reign of Pippin IV*, is easily dismissed as a pleasant, quickly dated comedy that has its heart in the right place.

I   Sweet Thursday (1954)

In the least successful of the three novels, *Sweet Thursday*, Steinbeck returned for the only time in his career to the setting of a former novel, employing many of the characters and places from *Cannery Row*. Although Doc is again the principal character, Steinbeck did not try to convert him from a passive philosopher into an activist. The "do-gooding" in the novel is assigned to two of the least credible characters Steinbeck ever created—Old Jingleballicks, a vulgar caricature of a philanthropist who finally gets Doc an appropriate job, and Hazel, a dim-witted character resurrected from *Cannery Row* to play a heavy-handed cupid.

Understandably exhausted by the monumental effort of producing *East of Eden,* Steinbeck turned in this next work to providing a libretto for one of the popular Rodgers and Hammerstein musical dramas that dominated the post–World War II Broadway stage. Many passages in *Sweet Thursday,* especially those in which Doc meditates on his loneliness, sound like the kind of talked-to-music soliloquies that the gifted team had introduced in *Carousel.* Even though *Pipe Dream,* the musical that developed from *Cannery Row* and *Sweet Thursday,* was not so successful as some of its creators' other ventures, the tuneful work provides a relaxing evening's entertainment. Unsupported by the music, however, *Sweet Thursday* is distressingly thin fare from a writer who had produced such robust chefs d'oeuvre as Steinbeck had.

Except for a droll account early in the novel of the Los Angeles Police Department's inability to discover that the marijuana flooding the city is being cultivated in the palm pots in a public plaza, the only fresh material in the novel is a spiteful attack on an ambitious young writer named Joe Elegant, whose nightmarish Gothic conceptions and daydreams of publicity stunts make him sound like the young Truman Capote. The two most amusing chapters in the novel, "The Great Roque War" and "The Pacific Grove Butterfly Festival" are malicious attacks on the specious moralism and literal-mindedness of the Methodist seaside camp-meeting community where Steinbeck had lived for a few years; but he had been attacking it since *To a God Unknown.*

Some sharp barbs are also aimed at "committee-mindedness," which suggest that Steinbeck's anger had a personal origin. The most pointed of these attacks is a speech to Doc by Old Jingleballicks, whom Steinbeck seems to have modeled on Little Orphan Annie's Daddy Warbucks:

"The only creative thing we have is the individual, but the law doesn't permit me to give money to an individual. I must give it to a group, an organization—and the only thing a group has ever created is book-keeping. . . . Why, if you through creative work should win a prize, most of the money would go in taxes. I don't mind taxes, God knows! But I do mind the kind of law that makes of charity not the full warmness of sharing but a stinking expediency" (184).[1]

These attacks on "group creation" had already appeared in *East of Eden* and in *Journal of a Novel*, in which Steinbeck writes that "there are no good collaborations," a curious remark from a friend of Richard Rodgers.

Sweet Thursday reworks—once more hopefully for the stage—the thesis of *Burning Bright* that consciousness is blighted without affection. When Doc returns from a long tour of army duty in World War II to resume work in his laboratory, he starts to write a paper about hysterical behavior in octopi; but he finds that he is too lonely to keep going, even though the only reason for the loss of the serenity that he possessed earlier in *Cannery Row* seems to be the demands of the plot of the novel. His friends, who in the earlier novel had tried to honor him with some disastrous parties, try this time to unite him with Suzy, a girl who has not been very successful in the local whorehouse. Both Suzy and Doc are highly self-conscious people, who know very well what they are doing; but both are too proud and narrowly self-reliant to recognize how much they need each other. When the simple-minded Hazel breaks Doc's arm with a baseball bat and Suzy has to drive his car on a collecting expedition for him, the emergency makes the pair realize their need for each other. "There are some things a man can't do alone. . . . without love," a "seer" tells Doc early in the novel, thereby providing the keynote for the book; but even this character is resurrected from *To a God Unknown*, as becomes evident when he tells Doc, "I have to go to the sunset now. I've come to the point where I don't think it can go down without me. That makes me seem needed" (73). (In the earlier novel, an old man sacrifices a small animal each sunset. When "the perfect time" comes, he him-self "will go over the edge of the world with the sun.")

Steinbeck's long-running attack on middle-class respectabil-ity also reaches an absurd climax in the portrayal of Fauna, the madame of the Bear Flag Restaurant, who spends off-duty hours teaching her girls etiquette and pointing proudly to a display of gold stars on the wall: "Every one of them stars represents a young lady from the Bear Flag that... married well. . . . Third from the end is president of the Salinas Forward and Upward Club and held the tree on Arbor Day" (94). Such sentimental glorification of the social outcast overshoots its mark by making the satire as two-dimensional as the behavior it satirizes—a practice that Steinbeck himself ridicules in "How to Tell Good Guys from Bad Guys," an often reprinted essay on the threat posed during the 1950s by Senator Joseph McCarthy. *Sweet Thursday* proves a patchwork quilt of reworked materials that pushes the eccentricities of its characters to the point that they possess no recognizably universal traits. If *Burning Bright* is too abstract and bloodless, *Sweet Thursday* is too specific and private.

II The Short Reign of Pippin IV

Certainly the attempt to return to a California setting that Steinbeck had lost touch with is one reason for the phoniness of *Sweet Thursday*. When the novelist set his next fable in a France with which he had been becoming increasingly familiar during the 1950s, he produced in *The Short Reign of Pippin IV* a work that, although slight, is his most consistently unified since *The Pearl* and his wittiest satire—except for isolated passages in longer works—since "Saint Katy the Virgin."

According to this tale, after one of the political crises that France underwent frequently during the late 1940s and 1950s, the monarchy is restored; and Pippin Heristal, a descendant of Charlemagne and amateur astronomer, ascends the throne. For a while the monarchy proves a tourist attraction, but Pippin begins to take his job too seriously and lectures the nation on needed reforms. With Pippin, the journalist in Steinbeck —hitherto rigorously excluded from his imaginative works —begins to take over the story with the result that he produces his most effective novel in a decade. Pippin's reform program, a document unprecedented in Steinbeck's fictional writings, reads much like the remedies that Steinbeck himself suggested in his newspaper stories for California's labor problems in the 1930s, and serves very well as an illustration of the author's personal convictions as a Stevensonian Democrat:

The first section dealt with taxes—to be kept as low as possible and to be collected from all.

The second, wages—to be keyed to profit and to move up and down with the cost of living.

Prices—to be strictly controlled against manipulation.

Housing—existing housing to be improved and new construction to be undertaken with supervision as to quality and rents.

The fifth section called for a reorganization of government to the end that it perform its functions with the least expenditure of money and personnel.

The sixth considered public health insurance and retirement pensions.

The seventh ordered the break-up of great land holdings to restore the wasted earth to productivity.

Although the criticism is ostensibly of France, much of it clearly applies to the smugly complacent United States of the Eisenhower years, also the target of many direct attacks in the novel. Fashionable literary taste is burlesqued again: Pippin's one daughter Clothilde, who has leaped to prominence at the age of sixteen on the strength of a novel *Adieu Ma Vie*, is clearly modeled on Françoise Sagan whose *Bonjour, Tristesse* had made her an overnight celebrity.

This timely novel is probably one of Steinbeck's most ephemeral because only a generation later it needs heavy annotation to be fully appreciated. Yet the work is important for three reasons: first, as an indication that its author could still under sufficient immediate prompting command a light, witty, biting prose and comment trenchantly on contemporary foibles; second, as a record of Steinbeck's mildly liberal political views that placed a heavy emphasis upon equality of opportunity and preservation of individual initiative; third, as an evidence of Steinbeck's continued insistence that the man who consciously and thoughtfully does what he believes is right—even if it isn't popular—because of genuine affection for his people deserves the heroic stature assigned Pippin, who, bereft of his crown, returns fittingly to his star gazing.

III *"How Mr. Hogan Robbed a Bank"*

An even more accomplished work is the short story "How Mr. Hogan Robbed a Bank" that appeared in the *Atlantic Monthly* in March, 1956. This story is the last piece of truly vintage Steinbeck that exemplifies the ironic mode of storytelling that was especially highly regarded during the years immediately after World War II when the "New Criticism" flourished. The story, a miniature drama of consciousness that makes no real point about the morality of bank robbing, demonstrates that careful observation pays because most people's thoughts and actions fall into ruts.

Mr. Hogan, a grocery clerk, develops the theory that bank robbers are caught because they indulge in too much hankypanky. For a year he schemes to rob the bank next to the grocery on the Saturday night before Labor Day; and when his plans work out exactly right, he steals eight thousand three hundred and twenty dollars, which he hides in the lining of a case that holds, ironically, his Knight Templar's uniform, an emblem of purity and good deeds. He distributes immediately only two five-dollar bills: one to his son, who has won an honorable mention in William Randolph Hearst's "I Love America" essay contest; and the other to his daughter, who has been a good sport about not winning an award. In this tale, tersely told from the same kind of no-nonsense viewpoint with which Hogan approaches the bank robbery, Steinbeck's only editorial comment is that "Mr. Hogan was a man who noticed things, and when it came to robbing a bank, this trait stood him in good stead." Other people do not notice things: "It was hot that summer, and people were irritated with it and anxious to get out of town, although the country was just as hot. They didn't think of that." In the furor following the robbery, neither do they think of the familiar figure of Mr. Hogan next door—an alert consciousness, unbothered by scruples, can easily exploit those whose thought patterns have become stereotyped.

IV   The Winter of Our Discontent

Many of the details from the Hogan story reappear six years later in the last novel Steinbeck published during his lifetime, *The Winter of Our Discontent*; but both the circumstances and the tone are much changed in the treatment of these details. Again the bank robbery is planned, but this time it never occurs, and mention of it could easily have been dropped altogether from a story cluttered with plots and subplots. Reworking his material, Steinbeck evidently was attacked again by the same scruples that had overwhelmed him when he was working on *The Grapes of Wrath*, so that the Hogan story—which is surely a "smart-alec" work of a kind rare among Steinbeck's publications—stands in the same relationship to this last novel that "L'Affaire Lettuceberg" must have to *The Grapes of Wrath*. Steinbeck could not finally let his self-conscious hero become a self-satisfied confidence man; the author had to make one last effort to put consciousness at the service of a conscience directed by affection. And the result is that sentimentality replaces satire.

"Did you know what you were doing?," Mr. Baker, the town banker, asks grocery clerk Ethan Allen Hawley as *The Winter of Our Discontent* lurches convulsively towards its soggy conclusion. Actually this question is what all of Steinbeck's devil's advocates have been asking his protagonists since La Santa Roja confronted Henry Morgan in *Cup of Gold*. An honest answer to the question provides, of course, the principal basis for determining whether the novel built around the character will be Naturalistic or a drama of consciousness.

This banker—fleshed out from the anonymous figure that Mr. Hogan robs in the short story—has a particular stake in the answer to this question because he has been outsmarted by the seemingly guileless Ethan Hawley. What the banker had not been able to achieve by duplicity, he is going to try to accomplish by making Hawley feel a shame that the banker himself does not have; but Ethan proves a match for this tactic. His dealings with the banker have had a long and dolorous history; in fact, his grandfather and the banker's father had once been partners in the whaling business; but, when the business declined, their last ship had burned in the harbor. The burning had prostrated the older Hawley—who could no more have killed a ship than a person—but it was hinted that the banker's father had committed arson to collect the insurance on the ship and to start a business with a brighter future. Later, the banker himself, a professed friend, had stood by and had seen Ethan's father squander the last of the family's fortune in bad investments. Although—perhaps because— Ethan himself has a singular reputation for honesty, he has lost ownership of the grocery store that he had stocked with the last of his patrimony; and he has been reduced to working as the clerk-manager for the Italian immigrant who has taken over the business.

This lurid history of the relationships between families that still go to church and take tea together provides the background for the reader's understanding Ethan's reasons for raising early in the novel the question, "Wouldn't it be true that any kindness in a money man would be a weakness?" Recognizing after three generations that his family has failed by answering "no," to this question, but that the banker's family has flourished by answering "yes," Ethan decides to scuttle tradition and join the opposition. The novel is an account of the awakening of his consciousness and the consequences thereof. "The new Ethan Allen Hawley," he proclaims, "goes along with the national follies and uses them when he can."

We find it difficult to fathom, however, just what "national follies" Ethan uses in his belated drive for dollars because the bank robbery that Mr. Hogan affected by reversing stereotyped expectations has no parallel in the novel. Hawley's success arises from settling two uniquely personal scores: (1) suspecting that his employer may have entered the country illegally, he tips off immigration officials anonymously and gets the store back—ironically, as a gift for faithful service —when the Italian is deported; (2) identifying the only field near his hometown of New Baytown suitable for an airport, he outwits the banker in the battle for its possession.

This field has belonged to Hawley's former close friend, almost brother, Danny Taylor, who has turned alcoholic after being inexplicably expelled from the Naval Academy (because Steinbeck hints, of gambling). Rather than feeling flushed with success at these coups, Hawley feels so terrible about his exploitation of those who have loved and trusted him that he starts to drown himself. He changes his mind at the last moment, however, not by analyzing his behavior and realizing that his suicide would benefit only his opponents, but because a family "talisman" he finds in his pocket reminds him that, even though the "light" has gone out in his life, he must continue to live to protect his young, sleepwalking daughter, "else another light might go out." Affection carries the day, and Ethan Allen Hawley finally achieves for Steinbeck the long-sought fusion of consciousness and conscience by deciding to live humbly with the hope—one that Sinclair Lewis's Babbitt had expressed forty years earlier—that things might be better for the next generation.

In J. D. Salinger's *The Catcher in the Rye*, a drunken former teacher tells Holden Caulfield that Wilhelm Stekel has said that, "The mark of the immature man is that he wants to die nobly for a cause, while the mark of the mature man is that he wants to live humbly for one." The last episode of *The Winter of Our Discontent* presents, in Stekel's terms, the miraculously sudden maturing of Ethan Allen Hawley.[2] The daughter, for whose sake Hawley decides he must live, shows, by the way, signs of being able to maintain the kind of integrity that Hawley feels he has surrendered when she anonymously informs the sponsors of Hearst's "I Love America" essay contest that her brother, who has won an honorable mention, had cribbed his essay from old speeches of Henry Clay and other dishonored dead.

On close scrutiny, Steinbeck's last novel published during his life proves to have many similarities to his first one, *Cup of Gold*. Repeatedly, he stresses that both the Hawleys and the banker's family had originally made their fortunes by piracy—dignified with the name of "privateering"—just as Morgan had. They had profited by gambling, by taking risks; and Hawley frequently muses that his own comparative failure has been simply the result of his unwillingness to take such risks. "Suppose my humble and interminable clerkship was not virtue at all," he asks himself, "but a moral laziness?"

He has prided himself on being "his brother's keeper," but he has found this course unprofitable. But, when he changes tactics, he feels that he has "poisoned" the money that he has given Danny Taylor—ostensibly to cure his alcoholism but really, as both realize, to drink himself to death. Ethan's interview with the banker reenacts Morgan's with La Santa Roja. After the pirate, like Ethan, has been responsible for the death of his closest friend, he informs the woman that she must return to her husband. "What have I to do with right, now—or reason, or logic, or conscience?" Morgan asks himself. "I want this money. I want security and comfort, and I have the power between my hands to take both. It may not be the ideal of youth, but I think it has been the world's practice from the beginning."

Hawley cannot, however, maintain this cynical stance. Just as Morgan recognizes that he has no more lusts and that his "desires are dry and rattling," Hawley feels that his light has

gone out and that there's "nothing blacker than a wick." Like
Morgan, Hawley has realizes that "civilization will split up
a character, and he who refuses to split goes under." The
civilization that the banker represents has surely "split up"
Hawley's character; but, unlike Morgan (created by a young
Steinbeck), Hawley (created by an aging Steinbeck) finds it
impossible to bounce back from the adjustments demanded
by this split. He almost literally "goes under" as he offers
himself to the rising tide in New Baytown harbor, just as he
has figuratively given himself up to the rising tide of commercial cupidity in the community. At the last minute, however,
Hawley recognizes that he is, if not his brother's keeper, at
least his daughter's. The ending of *The Winter of Our Discontent* resembles neither that of *Cup of Gold* nor that of any
other of Steinbeck's works; it is like that of Willa Cather's
The Professor's House, in which another man in whom "a
light" has burned recognizes that his labors of love have only
isolated him from his socially and financially ambitious family.
Professor St. Peter also flirts with suicide, but he recognizes
that "He had never learned to live without delight. And he
would have to learn to.... Theoretically, he knew that life
is possible, may be even pleasant, without joy, without passionate griefs. But it had never occurred to him that he might
have to live like that." Nor has it occurred to Ethan Allen
Hawley, who is also going to have to live henceforth without
joy.

Similarities between Willa Cather's apprentice novel *Alexander's Bridge* and her mature triumph *The Professor's House*
were noted by James E. Miller, Jr., in an address to the Willa
Cather Centennial Seminar. Willa Cather and John Steinbeck
had much in common: both came from farm communities not
far removed from frontier conditions; both early exhibited artistic tendencies that isolated them from their surroundings; and
both set much of their most prized fiction—Willa Cather's *My
Ántonia* and *O Pioneers!*; Steinbeck's *The Red Pony* and *Of
Mice and Men*—in places that they had known as children.
Later, both migrated to the big city and eventually found homes
there; and both experienced vast disillusionments that resulted
in their work coming back full circle in *The Professor's House*
and in *The Winter of Our Discontent* to the initial despair
also reflected in Mark Twain's *Huckleberry Finn.* While Cather

completed the cycle more quickly and went on to gain from the contemplation of history a new serenity in *Death Comes for the Archbishop* and *Shadows on the Rock*, Steinbeck apparently never found the same relief, though he sought it in his efforts to modernize Malory. Both these prodigious children of the farm frontier blamed the aspiration for worldly things that was inspired by an urban, commercial civilization for the death of a dream of personal integrity.

In *The Winter of Our Discontent*, Steinbeck did at last create the novel to which each reader could respond in terms of his own bias; but the author's bias is apparent. When civic officials are accused in the novel of various malpractices that appear trivial by standards established by our later governors, Hawley observes that perhaps it's "everybody's crime." The question Steinbeck never asked is whether his banker's behavior and practices are truly representative of "civilization," though they might so strike an awestruck farmboy arrived in the big city. Although Steinbeck wrote in one of his "Letters to Alicia," "I don't like any government of any kind and I only accept what I have to because it makes me safer and more comfortable," he was outraged when governments failed to function as well as they might.[3] He never captured Thoreau's concept of government as only an "expedient"; nor had he—as his restless traveling in his later years indicates—developed Thoreau's ability to "travel much in Concord." At the two finest moments in his fiction, he endowed Tom Joad and Doc of *Cannery Row* with an ability to transcend their material situations that can only be called "mystical"; but he had not quite reached this state himself, and he had not been able to summon a concept of it when he urgently needed it for this last novel. Except for a few moments in his life, something existed in Steinbeck of the little girl who told the interviewers for *The Lonely Crowd* that she would like to be able to fly like Superman "if everybody else did." Maybe his shared fear of "conspicuousness" is one of the qualities that made him such a popular author.

Perhaps in *The Winter of Our Discontent* he did not write Everyman's story—if there is such a story—but he may have given final form to the favorite story of a postfrontier generation—a story that insists with a kind of Arthurian guilelessness that the development of consciousness must be accompanied by an equal development of conscience or else a light goes out. The grim moral of *The Winter of Our Discontent* is that a man can't beat the connivers—"the little foxes"; he can only outfox them at the price of his personal integrity. Like T. S. Eliot's speaker in "Gerontion," Steinbeck ends asking, "After such knowledge, what forgiveness?"[4] The very question that perplexes those post–World War II writers that Jerry Bryant discusses in *The Open Decision*—"Can't we expect more from consciousness than guilt?"—plagued Steinbeck. If the Nobel Prize committee recognized—as its statement suggests it may have—that even in this last fiction Steinbeck recorded accurately the doubts and equivocations of his generation (and of several preceding American generations that had lamented the loss of a frontier), it made an award as deserved as any other.

CHAPTER 12

John Steinbeck and the American Consciousness

URING the late 1950s, when Steinbeck expressed in writings like *The Short Reign of Pippin IV* and "How Mr. Hogan Robbed a Bank" a cynicism that had been missing from his work since the late 1920s, he contributed to Hugh Hefner's *Playboy* magazine (which was constantly seeking to enhance its image by counterbalancing risqué cartoons with think-pieces by celebrated writers) his most mordant fiction, "The Short-Short Story of Mankind," an exercise in the vein of the then-fashionable "black humor" of J. P. Donleavy, Joseph Heller, and other writers.

The story of mankind, according to Steinbeck, is an unending cycle of frustration and remorse. Repeatedly, anyone who makes a substantial contribution to bettering the human condition is quickly eliminated by outraged elders as a threat to the status quo, although he is subsequently deified by those who enjoy his contributions without having to put up with him. People, Steinbeck concludes, refuse to change until they face extinction. Then they do something about the situation:

It isn't any goodness of heart and we may not want to go ahead but right from the cave time we've had to choose and so far we've never chose extinction. It'd be kind of silly if we killed ourselves off after all this time. If we do, we're stupider than the cave people and I don't think we are. I think we're just exactly as stupid and that's pretty bright in the long run.[1]

This cynical philosophy is quite similar to that of a character named Dr. Gillies in Thornton Wilder's novel *The Eighth Day*: "He had no doubt that the coming century would be too direful to contemplate—that is to say, like all the other centuries. . . . There are no Golden Ages and Dark Ages. There is the ocean-like monotony of the generations of men under the alternations of fair and foul weather." The concept that man has not basi-

cally improved since prehistoric times is hard to identify, however, with the John Steinbeck who could a few years after
publishing "The Short-Short Story of Mankind" affirm in his
Nobel Prize acceptance speech that "a writer who does not
passionately believe in the perfectibility of man has no dedication nor any membership in literature."

The clash between these two positions reflects a tension
that persists throughout Steinbeck's career. Philosophically,
he wished to believe in man's perfectibility, but his fictions
often denied this possibility. Many of his stories embody a
defeatist philosophy that he denounces in his editorial writings. Only in *The Grapes of Wrath* does the artist illustrate
the views of the commentator. (In *The Red Pony* and *Cannery
Row*, the often irrepressible commentator is mercifully
silenced.) Perhaps creative writers are wisest to be heard only
through their fiction. Where fiction conveys a message (and
it must almost unavoidably speak of man's fate), we must draw
from it the message that it presents and not attempt to read
into it—even at the author's behest—ideas that cannot be found
there.

In the autobiographical *In Touch*, Steinbeck's son, John IV,
comments that his father "seems to have become a kind of
American-conscience figure." We need read only *America and
Americans* and "Letters to Alicia" to agree that Steinbeck
sometimes sought such a role; and for many people, he may
have achieved it, although his writings about the Viet Nam
conflict late in his life often found him truculently isolated
from fellow artists. This characterization of the writer as "conscience figure," however, is likely to obscure the truly distinctive thing about novelists in general and about Steinbeck in
particular—they often make their poorest showings in such
a role.

Although fiction writers may concern themselves with
morals, such concern is not their unique or even their primary
function. Henry James provides the classic analysis of the
artist's role in his essay "The Art of Fiction"—"questions of
art are questions (in the widest sense) of execution; questions
of morality are quite another affair." Earlier in the essay, James
comments that, if the reader doesn't see something, "This is
exactly what the artist who has reasons of his own for thinking
he *does* see it undertakes to show [the reader]." Art helps

man *see,* as nothing else can. As man's vision improves, so *may* his morals. As I have observed in the discussion of Steinbeck's final novels in chapter 11, it is naïve to equate the development of man's heart and spirit with the development of man's mind. As Henry James—and Edgar Allan Poe before him in a review of Hawthorne's *Twice-Told Tales*—perceived, the writer must make the reader see before beginning to tell the reader how to act or how to think about what he sees. Writing that seeks to instruct before it illuminates is lifeless dogma.

Art is, therefore, more a matter of consciousness than of conscience; and I think that we can best understand Steinbeck's successes if we think of him as a master of the American consciousness who has helped his countrymen to see just about as much as they have been able to. Conversely, we can best understand his failures as examples of a penchant for moralizing causing him to lose touch with the perceptions of his senses. His works like *Burning Bright* that have addressed themselves almost exclusively to the audiences' consciences rather than their consciousnesses have been his least well received.

His failure to function most effectively as a conscience figure is suggested by his feeling compelled to preface his last novel, *The Winter of Our Discontent,* with the injunction that "readers seeking to identify the fictional people and places here described would do better to inspect their own communities and search their own hearts, for this book is about a large part of America today." If a novel succeeds in speaking to readers about their own condition, the novelist does not need to tell them that it does; if readers are more interested in discovering what particular persons and places are concealed behind fictions, the fiction has made them *see* the characters and settings more clearly than any principles they embody. The writer has confused his private opinions with universal truth, as I have previously suggested Steinbeck did when he concocted the Trask family allegory for *East of Eden.* Steinbeck was at his best when he made readers see the world (especially the fading twilight world of "The Leader of the People" and *Cannery Row* and the Hamilton family story in *East of Eden*) rather than when he set about reforming it by turning oriental savants loose on Biblical texts in *East of Eden* or sending trapeze artists to sea in *Burning Bright*. He wisely omitted from *The Grapes of Wrath* the kind of programs for action to relieve the plight of the migrant workers in California that he spelled out in his earlier newspaper stories. He might have profited in his subsequent fiction from more often following his own example.

A novel that narrates an action (some recent novels don't, but Steinbeck admits in *Journal of a Novel* that he writes "old-fashioned" works) casts a principal actor against some kind of obstacle. The basic argument of this study of Steinbeck has been that if the actor is not aware of the nature of the obstacle or lacks the requisites for consciously coping with it, the work may be called *Naturalistic*; whereas if the actor is conscious of the nature of the obstacle and exercises responsible choice in dealing with it—whether or not he succeeds in his struggle—the work is a *drama of consciousness.*

A Naturalistic fiction may end comically (really melodramatically) if the actor gets around the obstacle (often through the intervention of a deus ex machina) or simply adjusts to living with it without ever really understanding it; it may end tragically (or we may prefer to say, pathetically) if the actor is defeated or destroyed by the obstacle. Dramas of consciousness may likewise end comically or tragically (we prefer usually to reserve these descriptions for those works in which the principal actors appear to know what they are doing), but there also exists the alternative possibility—not available in a Naturalistic situation—that the actor may transcend his previous situation by consciously discovering that what seemed an obstacle was actually not one at all, so that he can go over it or through it rather than being obliged to go around it or be stopped by it. Such an action may be called *epic*—it creates a new world instead of dealing in some fashion with an old one. I think that these distinctions may be used to group Steinbeck's fictions and to develop some hypotheses about the often discussed "rise" and "decline" in their artistic quality.

Steinbeck's earliest surviving works, *Cup of Gold* and *To a God Unknown*, are both fables of conscious actors who recognize the nature of the obstacles confronting them and take conscious responsibility for dealing with them: Henry Morgan in *Cup of Gold* achieves a selfish triumph, and Joseph Wayne in *To a God Unknown* selflessly sacrifices himself to the common good. Both the cynical comedy and the mystical tragedy are products of a pervasive mentality of the Waste Land years of the 1920s that is summarized in T. S. Eliot's line in "Gerontion": "What is kept must be adulterated." Morgan splits up before civilization; Wayne keeps his purity only by giving up his life.

Steinbeck's next five major works are Naturalistic, and four of them are harrowingly pathetic. *The Red Pony*, which may have been the earliest conceived, is a rare example of a Naturalistic work in which melodrama is elevated into spiritual comedy when a growing boy learns to live with natural obstacles without being able to overcome them. Jody Tiflin cannot transcend his material condition, but he can and does transcend the psychological frustrations that have relegated his elders to "oaths and walking-sticks." In *The Pastures of Heaven, Tortilla Flat, In Dubious Battle,* and *Of Mice and Men* (as well as in many of the stories collected in *The Long Valley*), the actors' aspirations outrun their abilities, and they are destroyed either physically or spiritually by forces that they cannot understand or control.

The Grapes of Wrath apparently was begun as still another novel of this kind; but some experience caused the author to change his mind, scrap his original manuscript, and turn his story into one of the few great epic accounts of the transcendence of the human spirit over material obstacles. The Joad family develops from a clan of Naturalistic characters who are seemingly doomed to the same dismal fates as the characters in Steinbeck's immediately preceding novels into a self-aware force that, after perceiving that the obstacles to its growth are internal rather than external, consciously chooses to live the life of the spirit rather than of the body, even though the physical problems facing the family have not been solved; and the author leaves the solution of that problem—if there is to be one—to the readers. Just as the Joads transcend themselves, Steinbeck himself had transcended what had previously seemed to be, and what were to become again, his limitations as a novelist by suggesting the possibility of a kind of perfectibility without prescribing the method of its achievement. Unfortunately, most readers missed the allegory and read this epic of the human spirit as fictionalized sociology. Always hypersensitive to public reactions, Steinbeck did not move beyond the peak he had attained in *The Grapes of Wrath*; instead he moved back to where he figured the public might be and began, with his visits to President Roosevelt, to advise people rather than illuminate them.

In his next three brief works—*The Forgotten Village, The Moon Is Down,* and *Bombs Away*—he presented self-conscious actors devising practical solutions to specific situations of immediate significance. For once, he was a good prophet: the American war effort produced the same good results as the actions in his fiction. Prophesying the historical turn of events, however, does not necessarily add to one's artistic stature. Too exclusive preoccupation with such expedient solutions to pressing immediate problems as supporting medical education and training bomber crews may actually hamper one's perception of universals.

Depressed by what he saw of World War II, Steinbeck fortunately withdrew from solving society's immediate problems and turned in *Cannery Row* to the timeless world of the cosmic Monterey. Through his portrayal of Doc, modeled on his friend Ed Ricketts, Steinbeck created at last the comedy of the human spirit that consciously accepts the natural limitations placed upon man as a physical being, but learns also to transcend them psychically through the arts. *Cannery Row* works—as few fictions have—at that precise line between comedy and epic at which the principal actor is more than an ordinary man without becoming a superman. *Cannery Row*, far from being a light or trivial book, is Steinbeck's triumph, even though its gentle message is harder to hear than the thunderous affirmation of *The Grapes of Wrath,* because it is the only work in which Steinbeck successfully embodies the conception that the contemplation of art can free man from the petty frustrations of the workaday world.

An artist cannot be faulted for failing to maintain or pass beyond the illumination that floods the last pages of *Cannery Row*—Steinbeck's radiant sunset to match the sunrise of *The Red Pony*. Probably in the evening of his talent, he should have stayed with journalism, but he was driven to keep trying to achieve something new, different, better. In his next three works—*The Pearl, The Wayward Bus,* and *Burning Bright*—he sought to create a Naturalistic figure who could serve as an :dequate principal actor in a cosmic drama of consciousness.

I have the feeling that merely identifying the quest suggests that a search—begun long before Steinbeck's time—for the person who is just "naturally" good, aware, and intelligent is futile. As much as men have wanted to believe in the existence of the noble savage, and as often as even the most enlightened systems of education have failed to produce fair and wise men, there has never been any evidence unearthed that people can hope to become just and wise without some kind of rigorous education that makes possible at last what Plato in his Socratic dialogues called "the examined life."

For John Steinbeck, *East of Eden* was the consummation of the effort to find a hero among the folk—a magnificent effort at a second epic to match *The Grapes of Wrath*. But, curiously, the folk-shaman, Samuel Hamilton, could not heal his own people, and it was left to a group of mandarin intellectuals to solve the secret of the meaning of *timshel* and to pass their wisdom to a group of symbol people, the Trasks, who did not create the arguments the book embodied, but were created to project the arguments.

Abandoning the search for the self-conscious folk-hero (most successful in the pseudohistorical film *Viva Zapata!*), Steinbeck turned in his three final fictions to comic portrayals of those who consciously accept their worlds as they find them; but nothing basically new is found in these books. *Sweet Thursday*—Steinbeck's only attempt to write a sequel—is a clumsy effort beside *Cannery Row*. *The Short Reign of Pippin IV* is delightful journalism, but already Steinbeck's most dated book. *The Winter of Our Discontent* is the tarnished Cup of Gold of the post–World War II Waste Land. Steinbeck displays after 1945 a consciousness unequal to the new demands made upon it by a changing society.

Yet Steinbeck could not "rest from travel," either actual physical travel, to see new lands or rediscover long-known ones, or new creative ventures. The quoted phrase is from Alfred Tennyson's poem "Ulysses," which Steinbeck asked to have read at his funeral service. The choice is understandable, because Steinbeck's vision was the vision of Tennyson's monologuist: "All experience is an arch wherethro'/ Gleams that untravell'd world." In Steinbeck's best moments he caught glimpses of that untraveled world, and even in his less inspired he did more to awaken the American consciousness to conditions along our national roads than any of his contemporaries succeeded in doing.

His best works remain those in which self-conscious characters transcend the frustrations of their environments—*The Red Pony, The Grapes of Wrath, Cannery Row,*—for these are the only novels in which Steinbeck becomes a timeless artist rather than an American seer. We must recognize that all three arose from personal crises—*The Red Pony,* from his first experience with death in the family;[2] *The Grapes of Wrath,* from his revulsion at betraying his own aims as a writer; *Cannery Row,* from his disheartenment caused by his observations of World War II. Perhaps circumstances did not at other times screw his faculties to their toughest effort. Reading *Journal of a Novel,* we wonder how someone as submerged as Steinbeck then was in the trivia of daily living managed to produce any novel.

His next best works are those early ones from *The Pastures of Heaven* to *Of Mice and Men,* in which he presents the pathetic defeats of Naturalistic characters. As "The Short-Short Story of Mankind" suggests in contrast to the Nobel Prize acceptance speech, Steinbeck's often misanthropic views clash with his efforts to affirm man's creative capacity. In his journalistic writings, he was often affirmative, but many of the fictions that are likely to remain his most enduring suggest that he was actually trying to convince himself, as much as anyone else, by his affirmative proclamations and that—except in rare moments of illumination—what he actually *saw* made him apprehensive. Certainly our observation that his least successful works—*The Wayward Bus, Burning Bright,* and *The Winter of Our Discontent* (along with the Trask story in *East of Eden*)—are those which were spurred by a moralistic impulse to lecture suggests that when Steinbeck became too concerned with other people's consciences, he began to lose touch with his own consciousness. As I said in the conclusion to the previous version of this book, however, Steinbeck's "failures by no means cancel out his successes. The author of *The Pastures of Heaven, Tortilla Flat, In Dubious Battle, Of Mice and Men, The Red Pony, The Grapes of Wrath, Cannery Row,* and a dozen distinguished short stories cannot fail to occupy a high place among contemporary American writers." I need now only remove the word *contemporary.*

Notes and References

Chapter One

1. Peter Lisca reproduces parts of this letter written from California in June, 1938, in *The Wide World of John Steinbeck* (New Brunswick, N.J.; 1958, p. 147.

2. Reported in the *New York Times*, October 26, 1962, p. 12.

3. W. H. Auden, "Squares and Oblongs," *Poets at Work* (New York, 1948), p. 176.

4. *America and Americans* (New York, 1966), p. 59. Steinbeck provides even more details on his great-grandfather's mission in "Letters to Alicia," *Newsday*, February 12, 1966, p. 3-W. One with the great-grandfather's vision would not have been deterred by the Jews' having been dispersed from Palestine nearly two millennia earlier.

5. See Joseph Fontenrose, *John Steinbeck: An Introduction and Interpretation* (New York, 1963), pp. 1–3, for a fuller account of Steinbeck's family, compiled with the assistance of members of the family.

6. "The Making of a New Yorker," *New York Times Magazine*, February 1, 1953, VI, iii, 27. The article is part of a special supplement exploring in words and pictures the complex image of New York City.

7. Lewis Gannett, "Preface," *Cup of Gold* (New York, 1936), p. v.

8. See Herbert Kline, "On John Steinbeck," *Steinbeck Quarterly*, IV (Summer, 1971), 80–88, for the director's reminisences of his association with John Steinbeck and a history of the making and distribution of the film.

9. See Warren French, ed., *A Companion to "The Grapes of Wrath"* (New York, 1963), pp. 133–43, for an account of these "answers" to the novel.

10. Lisca, p. 197.

11. *Journal of a Novel: The "East of Eden" Letters* (New York, 1969), p. 180.

12. See Lawrence William Jones, "Random Thoughts from Paris: Steinbeck's *Un Américain à New York et à Paris*, *Steinbeck Quarterly*, III (Spring, 1970), 27–30, for a description of this book.

13. Reported in *New York Times*, June 23, 1957, p. 23.

Chapter Two

1. Edwin H. Cady, *The Light of Common Day: Realism in American Fiction* (Bloomington, Ind.; 1971), pp. 47, 45.

2. Lilian R. Furst and Peter N. Skrine, *Naturalism* (London, 1971), p. 70. Of Naturalism in the United States, Furst observes, "Inconclusive though it may seem, there is no alternative but to accept the fact that Naturalism in the U.S.A. was not primarily a literary concept" (36).

3. Charles Child Walcutt, *American Literary Naturalism: A Divided Stream* (Minneapolis, 1956), pp. 23–28.

4. Donald Pizer, *Realism and Naturalism in Nineteenth-Century American Literature* (Carbondale, Ill.; 1966), pp. 12–14.

5. Quoted in James E. Miller, Jr., ed., *Theory of Fiction: Henry James* (Lincoln, Nebr.; 1972), p. 163. Miller also reprints the comments on *drama of consciousness* from James's preface to *Roderick Hudson* (1907), pp. 163–64.

6. For a detailed analysis of *The Red Badge of Courage* as a novel exemplifying the transformation of *Naturalism* into *drama of consciousness*, consult Warren French's lecture in the "Cassette Curriculum," 19th Century American Writers series (Deland, Fla.; 1971).

Chapter Three

1. All page references are to *Cup of Gold* (New York, 1936—a reissuing of the very rare 1929 edition) and *To a God Unknown* (New York, dated 1933, but usually only available in the reissue of 1937).

2. Steinbeck's special definition of *nonteleological thinking* is based on his friend Ed Ricketts's theorizing and is most clearly explained by Richard Astro in *John Steinbeck and Edward F. Ricketts: The Shaping of a Novelist* (Minneapolis, 1973) as describing "an open approach to life by the man who looks at events and accepts them as such without reservation or qualification, and in so doing perceives the whole picture by becoming an identifiable part of that picture" (38).

3. Richard Astro draws detailed parallels between Hemingway's and Steinbeck's "wasteland" novels of the 1920s and 1930s in "Phlebas Sails the Caribbean," *The Twenties: Fiction, Poetry, Drama*, ed. by Warren French (Deland, Fla.; 1974). Astro reads *Cup of Gold* as "Steinbeck's critique of the solipsistic pursuit of wealth and empire" and finds its "real horror" in the novelist's finding "no satisfying options to Morgan's drive for power." Joseph Wayne in *To a God Unknown*, Astro argues, becomes "a true mythic hero."

4. Lawrence W. Jones, "A Note on Steinbeck's Earliest Stories," *Steinbeck Quarterly*, II (Fall, 1969), 60. Jones had not then located the story, which appears as "The Gifts of Iban" by John Stern in *The Smoker's Companion: A National Monthly for Hearth and Home*, March, 1927, pp. 18–19, 70–72. Preston Beyer has graciously supplied me with a facsimile copy of the rare original.

Chapter Four

1. Lisca, pp. 39–40. Lisca also mentions that Steinbeck intended to circulate another novel called "Dissonant Symphony" with *The Pastures of Heaven*, but withdrew it as "a mess" (58).

2. Astro, *John Steinbeck and Edward F. Ricketts*, p. 97.

3. Forrest L. Ingram, *Representative Short-Story Cycles of the Twentieth Century* (The Hague, 1971), p. 15. Ingram also includes a brief discussion of *The Pastures of Heaven*, pp. 39–43.

4. Because of the rarity of the original edition of *The Pastures of Heaven* (New York, 1932), page references are to the "new" Bantam Books paperback edition (New York, 1956).

5. Lisca, p. 93.

6. Howard Levant argues in "John Steinbeck's *The Red Pony*: A Study in Narrative Technique," *Journal of Narrative Technique*, I (May, 1971), 77–85, that "the major themes are always kept in view and focus the organic development of the narrative."

7. An unexpected controversy has arisen over the meaning and artistic success of this nearly flawlessly executed story. See reports in *American Literary Scholarship 1969* (Durham, N.C.; 1971), p. 217; *American Literary Scholarship 1970* (Durham, N.C.; 1972), p. 245, and *American Literary Scholarship 1971* (Durham, N.C., 1973), p. 233.

8. Maxwell Geismar, *Writers in Crisis: The American Novel Between Two Wars* (Boston, 1942), p. 255.

9. Arthur F. Kinney, "The Arthurian Cycle in *Tortilla Flat*," *Modern Fiction Studies*, XI (Spring, 1965), 11–20. Kinney's article can be recommended for the thoroughness of its study of the relationship of this novel to *Morte d'Arthur*.

10. Howard Levant, "*Tortilla Flat*: The Shape of John Steinbeck's Career," *PMLA*, LXXXV (October, 1970), 1087–95.

11. See Warren French, *The Social Novel at the End of an Era* (Carbondale, Ill.; 1966) for an account of Steinbeck's relationship to the "back-to-the-farm" literature of the Depression years.

Chapter Five

1. Page references to the original edition of *In Dubious Battle* (New York, 1936) are also correct for the Modern Library edition.

2. Peter Lisca, " 'The Raid' and *In Dubious Battle*," *Steinbeck Quarterly*, V (Summer-Fall, 1972), 90–94.

3. William R. Osborne points out and analyzes the differences in "The Texts of Steinbeck's 'The Chrysanthemums,' " *Modern Fiction Studies*, XII (Winter, 1966–67), 479–84.

4. Professor Simmonds has graciously provided me with a copy

of his unpublished article, "The Original Manuscripts of Steinbeck's 'The Chrysanthemums,' " upon which I have based these comments.

5. See Warren French, " 'Johnny Bear'—Steinbeck's 'Yellow Peril' Story," *Steinbeck Quarterly*, V (Summer-Fall, 1972), 101–7, for an extended discussion of the relationship of "Johnny Bear" to the anti-Chinese agitation in California between the Civil War and World War II.

6. *The "Log" from "The Sea of Cortez"* (New York, 1951), pp. xxiii–xxiv.

7. Richard Astro stresses in *John Steinbeck and Edward F. Ricketts*, however, that Steinbeck used Ricketts's nonteleological thinking "not as theme, but as fictional method" and that Steinbeck is at his best when he uses "the nonteleological approach as a means of handling the data of fiction" (106). This method permits Steinbeck to present human affairs as he believes they are while still expressing outrage that they are that way.

Chapter Six

1. Lisca, *The Wide World of John Steinbeck*, p. 147.

2. Page references are to *"The Grapes of Wrath": Text and Criticism*, edited by Peter Lisca (New York, 1972).

3. Lisca reprints in the edition cited in footnote 2 (pp. 858–59), a letter from Steinbeck to Pascal Covici, written early in 1939, in which Steinbeck defends the ending of the novel and observes that a reader will find as many "layers" as he can and "won't find more than he has in himself."

4. Frederic I. Carpenter, "The Philosophical Joads," *College English*, II (January, 1941), 25.

5. *The Forgotten Village* (New York, 1941), p. 5.

6. Translation follows C. H. Grandgent, *Dante* (New York, 1916), 273–75. For a fuller account of Dante's arguments and their application to an analysis of the layers of meaning in *The Grapes of Wrath*, see the chapter on this novel by Warren French in *A Study Guide to Steinbeck: A Handbook to His Major Works*, edited by Tetsumaro Hayashi (Metuchen, N.J.; 1974).

Chapter Seven

1. See Astro, *John Steinbeck and Edward F. Ricketts*, especially pages 12–19, for an account of the two men's respective contributions to the "Log" and the development of the "nonteleological thinking" expounded in it.

2. Astro, *John Steinbeck and Edward F. Ricketts*, p. 150.

3. Lisca, *The Wide World of John Steinbeck*, p. 187.

4. *Bombs Away: The Story of a Bomber Team* (New York, 1942), pp. 13–14.

Chapter Eight

1. Lisca, *The Wide World of John Steinbeck*, p. 212. Although a remarkable forerunner of the "black humor" of the 1960s, "The Time the Wolves Ate the Vice-Principal" has never been reincorporated into the novel and has appeared only obscurely in *'47 The Magazine of the Year*, I (March, 1947), 26–27.

Chapter Nine

1. Lawrence William Jones, *John Steinbeck as Fabulist* (*Steinbeck Monograph Series, No. 3*, Muncie, Ind.; 1973), p. 15.
2. Ibid., pp. 7–8.
3. Warren French and Walter Kidd, eds., *American Winners of the Nobel Literary Prize* (Norman, Okla.; 1968), p. 199.
4. *The "Log" from the "Sea of Cortez"* (New York, 1951), pp. 102–3.
5. Lisca, *The Wide World of John Steinbeck*, pp. 233–40.
6. Lester Jay Marks, *Thematic Design in the Novels of John Steinbeck* (The Hague, 1969), p. 108.
7. Lisca, *The Wide World of John Steinbeck*, p. 232.
8. Fontenrose, p. 110.
9. Robert Morsberger, "Steinbeck's Zapata: Rebel vs. Revolutionary," *Steinbeck: The Man and His Work*, ed. by Tetsumaro Hayashi and Richard Astro (Corvallis, Ore.; 1971), pp. 43–63.
10. Lisca, *The Wide World of John Steinbeck*, p. 258.

Chapter Ten

1. Page references in the text are to the first edition, *East of Eden* (New York, 1952).
2. Page references are to *Journal of a Novel: The "East of Eden" Letters* (New York, 1969).
3. Wayne C. Booth, *The Rhetoric of Fiction* (Chicago, 1961), p. 20. Booth begins the last paragraph of his opening chapter, "Telling and Showing," with the observation that "the author's judgment is always present." Steinbeck's problems arise when he does not accept consistent responsibility for his judgments.
4. John J. McAleer, "*An American Tragedy* and *In Cold Blood*," *Thought*, XLVII (1972), 569–86.

Chapter Eleven

1. Page references are to the first edition, *Sweet Thursday* (New York, 1954).

2. See Warren French, "Steinbeck's Winter Tale," *Modern Fiction Studies*, XI (Spring, 1965), 66–74, for further discussion of a number of parallels between *The Winter of Our Discontent* and J. D. Salinger's *The Catcher in the Rye* as explorations of sensitive persons' discontent with urban American civilization after World War II.

3. "Letters to Alicia," *Newsday*, December 24, 1965, p. 3-W.

4. See Donna Gerstenberger, "Steinbeck's American Waste Land," *Modern Fiction Studies*, XI (Spring, 1965), 59–65, for a discussion of T. S. Eliot's *The Waste Land* as Steinbeck's "frame of reference" for *The Winter of Our Discontent*. Gerstenberger concludes that solutions to the problems explored in both works "are no easier, it would seem, in 1961 than they were in 1922."

Chapter Twelve

1. "The Short-Short Story of Mankind," *Playboy*, April, 1958, p. 34.

2. See "My Short Novels," *Wings* [a monthly promotional publication of the Literary Guild], XXVI (October, 1953), 1–8, for Steinbeck's discussion of the inspiration for *The Red Pony*. This is one of a very few, uncharacteristic statements in which Steinbeck discusses the origins of one of his fictional works.

Selected Bibliography

PRIMARY SOURCES

Only separate books are listed. See Tetsumaro Hayashi, *A New Steinbeck Bibliography 1929–1971* (Metuchen, N.J.: Scarecrow Press, 1973) for a full list of American publications. Since it is difficult to draw a firm line between Steinbeck's fiction and nonfiction, the following division is between those primarily fictional narratives that are discussed in this book and those primarily personal reports that are beyond the scope of this book.

1. Fiction

Bombs Away: The Story of a Bomber Team. New York: Viking Press, 1942.
Burning Bright. New York: Viking Press, 1950.
Cannery Row. New York: Viking Press, 1945.
Cup of Gold. New York: Robert M. McBride & Co., 1929.
East of Eden. New York: Viking Press, 1952.
The Forgotten Village. New York: Viking Press, 1941.
The Grapes of Wrath. New York: Viking Press, 1939.
In Dubious Battle. New York: Covici, Friede, 1936.
The Long Valley. New York: Viking Press, 1938.
The Moon Is Down (novel). New York: Viking Press, 1942.
The Moon Is Down (play). New York: Viking Press, 1943.
Of Mice and Men (separate editions of novel and play). New York: Covici, Friede, 1937.
The Pastures of Heaven. New York: Brewer, Warren & Putnam, 1932.
The Pearl. New York: Viking Press, 1947.
The Red Pony. New York: Covici, Friede, 1937 [contains only three stories].
The Short Reign of Pippin IV. New York: Viking Press, 1957.
Sweet Thursday. New York: Viking Press, 1954.
To a God Unknown. New York: Robert O. Ballou, 1933.
Viva Zapata! (script of 1952 film). New York: Viking Press, 1974.
The Wayward Bus. New York: Viking Press, 1947.
The Winter of Our Discontent. New York: Viking Press, 1961.

2. Reports

America and Americans. New York: Viking Press, 1966.
Un Américain à New York et à Paris. Paris: Rene Julliard, 1956 (Contains some short fictions; French translation by Jean-Francois Rozan; no edition in English.)

180

Journal of a Novel: The "East of Eden" Letters. New York: Viking Press, 1969.

Once There Was a War. New York: Viking Press, 1958 (dispatches to the *New York Herald Tribune* in 1943, with a new introduction by the author).

A Russian Journal. New York: Viking Press, 1948.

Sea of Cortez, with Edward F. Ricketts. New York: Viking Press, 1941.

Speech Accepting the Nobel Prize for Literature. New York: Viking Press, 1962. Limited edition of 3200 copies, not for sale.

Their Blood Is Strong. San Francisco: Simon J. Lubin Society of California, 1938. Newspaper reports to the *San Francisco News* in 1936, with a new conclusion by the author.

Travels with Charley in Search of America. New York: Viking Press, 1962.

3. Adaptation

The Acts of King Arthur and His Noble Knights. Edited by Horton Chase. New York: Farrar, Straus and Giroux, 1976. An uncompleted modernization of Sir Thomas Malory's *Morte d'Arthur*, published posthumously.

SECONDARY SOURCES

Only books and collections of shorter pieces can be mentioned. For a detailed list of the extensive American criticism, consult Tetsumaro Hayashi, *A New Steinbeck Bibliography 1929–1971*, supplemented by *A New Steinbeck Bibliography 1971–1981* (Metuchen, N.J.: Scarecrow Press, 1983). For categorical evaluations of writings about Steinbeck, see Warren French, "John Steinbeck," in *Sixteen Modern American Authors*, ed. Jackson W. Bryer (Durham, N.C.: Duke University Press, 1974; with a supplementary volume in 1985) and the annual volumes of *American Literary Scholarship*, published since 1963 by Duke University Press.

1. Books

ASTRO, RICHARD. *John Steinbeck and Edward F. Ricketts: The Shaping of a Novelist.* Minneapolis: University of Minnesota Press, 1973. An analysis of the influence of Ricketts's philosophy on Steinbeck's fiction, drawing extensively upon Ricketts's unpublished essays.

BENSON, JACKSON J. *The True Adventures of John Steinbeck, Writer.* New York: Viking Press, 1984. The first adequate biography of John Steinbeck, a more than thousand-page study, dealing in particularly sympathetic detail with the novelist's formative years in California.

BURROWS, MICHAEL. *John Steinbeck and His Films.* St. Austell, Cornwall [England]: Primestyle, 1970. A collection of comments from many sources, accompanied by many still photographs from the films.

DeMott, Robert. *Steinbeck's Reading: A Catalogue of Books Owned and Borrowed.* New York: Garland, 1984. A list of all the books that Steinbeck is known to have owned or borrowed, with a long introductory essay on his reading tastes and extracts from his writings relating to the titles mentioned.

Ditsky, John. *Essays on "East of Eden."* Steinbeck Monograph Series, no. 7. Muncie, Ind.: John Steinbeck Society of America, 1977. A group of related analyses arguing for the importance of this long novel that had disappointed many other critics.

Fensch, Thomas. *Steinbeck and Covici: The Story of a Friendship.* Middlebury, Vt.: Erickson, 1979. A biography compiled from extracts from this important correspondence with Steinbeck's long-time editor, but with disappointingly little annotation.

Fontenrose, Joseph. *John Steinbeck: An Introduction and Interpretation.* New York: Barnes and Noble, 1963. A pioneering account of mythological materials influencing Steinbeck's fiction by a distinguished Classicist at the University of California–Berkeley, who knows the Steinbeck country well.

―――. *Steinbeck's Unhappy Valley: A Study of "The Pastures of Heaven."* Berkeley: Privately printed for the author, 1981. A meticulous examination and evaluation of all the thematic elements unifying this controversial "short-story cycle."

French, Warren. *A Filmguide to "The Grapes of Wrath."* Bloomington: Indiana University Press, 1973. An analysis of the celebrated film version as an unreliable adaptation of the novel and a cinematic classic in its own right.

Garcia, Reloy. *Steinbeck and D. H. Lawrence: Fictive Voices and the Ethical Imperative.* Steinbeck Monograph Series, no. 2. Muncie, Ind.: John Steinbeck Society of America, 1972. An elucidation of strikingly similar strengths and weaknesses in the fictional writings of these authors.

Gray, James. *John Steinbeck.* University of Minnesota Pamphlets on American Writers, no. 94. Minneapolis: University of Minnesota Press, 1971. A short tribute to Steinbeck's "story-telling skill," which describes him as a "moral ecologist, obsessively concerned with man's spiritual struggle to adjust to his environment."

Hayashi, Tetsumaro. *John Steinbeck: A Dictionary of His Fictional Characters.* Metuchen, N.J.: Scarecrow Press, 1976. An alphabetical finding list of all the identifiable characters in Steinbeck's writings.

Hedgepeth, Joel. "Ed Ricketts and John Steinbeck Explore the Pacific Coast"; "Breaking Through." In *The Outer Shores.* Eureka, Calif.: Mad River Press, 1978, 1979. An account by a long-time close friend of Steinbeck and Ricketts's investigations of the marine life of the Pacific littoral, followed by a summary of Ricketts's philosophical theorizings.

JONES, LAWRENCE WILLIAM. *John Steinbeck as Fabulist*. Edited by Marston LaFrance. Steinbeck Monograph Series, no. 3. Muncie, Ind.: John Steinbeck Society of America, 1973. An illumination of Steinbeck's increasing propensity for parable writing after World War II, utilizing the techniques for analyzing fiction developed by Sheldon Sacks in *Fiction and the Shape of Belief*.

KIERNAN, THOMAS. *The Intricate Music: A Biography of John Steinbeck*. Boston: Little, Brown, 1979. An early attempt to write a brief commercial biography of Steinbeck that has been superseded by Jackson J. Benson's biography mentioned above and other recent writings.

LEVANT, HOWARD. *The Novels of John Steinbeck*. Columbia: University of Missouri Press, 1974. A study of Steinbeck's fiction in terms of his use of "dramatic" and "panoramic" techniques, especially as these relate to his increasing problems in finding adequate fictional forms to embody his philosophy.

LISCA, PETER. *Nature and Myth*. New York: Crowell, 1978. Meditative reflections on Steinbeck's fiction by the author of the pioneering study of the novelist's work (see next entry), designed especially to interest young readers in Steinbeck's balancing of his observations of nature with his philosophical speculations.

————. *The Wide World of John Steinbeck*. New Brunswick, N.J.: Rutgers University Press, 1958. Although the biographical material in this pioneering study of Steinbeck's fiction has been incorporated into and expanded in later works, it remains important as the first major effort to assert Steinbeck's importance as an American novelist and to provide intensive New Critical analyses of his works.

McCARTHY, PAUL. *John Steinbeck*. New York: Ungar, 1980. Part of a series of brief, comprehensive monographs on modern authors that competently summarizes the principal critical positions taken during the first four decades of study of the novelist's work.

MARKS, LESTER JAY. *Thematic Design in the Novels of John Steinbeck*. New York: Mouton, 1969. An examination of the aesthetic resolution in the novels of three recurring patterns—man's need of a god, man viewed as "a group animal," and the "nonteleological" concept that the "very mystery of life" spurs the search for human values.

MILLICHAP, JOSEPH R., *Steinbeck and Film*. New York: Ungar, 1983. A thorough and forthright critique of the film versions of Steinbeck's works and their relationships to their sources and of the artistic value of his original contributions to the screen that advances the theory that his increasing involvement with Hollywood may have affected the quality of his later fictional work.

MOORE, HARRY THORNTON. *The Novels of John Steinbeck: A First Critical Study*. Chicago: Normandie House, 1939. Reprint. Port Washington, N.Y.: Kennikat Press, 1968. Written shortly after the publication of *The Grapes of Wrath* stimulated interest in Steinbeck's work, this

early study by a critic who later lost interest in Steinbeck provides
valuable insights into critical attitudes of the 1930s.

OWENS, LOUIS. *John Steinbeck's Re-vision of America.* Athens: University
of Georgia Press, 1985. Reviews intensively in terms of the American
dream, the California novels, which Owens regards as the "most ambitious and thorough examinations of the idea of America yet produced
by any writer."

PRATT, JOHN CLARK. *John Steinbeck: A Critical Essay.* Grand Rapids,
Mich.: Eerdmans, 1970. Part of a series on "Contemporary Writers in
Christian Perspectives," this pamphlet describes Steinbeck's use of
Christian elements in "syncretic allegories."

SIMMONDS, ROY S. *Steinbeck's Literary Achievement.* Steinbeck Monograph Series, no. 6. Muncie, Ind.: John Steinbeck Society of America,
1976. A brilliantly composed appreciation of Steinbeck's fiction that
provides the best introduction to the themes, characters, style, and
humor that are responsible for the unique quality of his writings.

STEINBECK, ELAINE, and ROBERT WALLSTEN, eds. *A Life in Letters.* New
York: Viking Press, 1975. A copious selection of extracts from John
Steinbeck's letters, with running editorial commentary and some selections from letters to Steinbeck, to provide a running record of the
writer's life in his own words, though heavily edited.

VALJEAN, NELSON. *John Steinbeck: The Errant Knight.* San Francisco:
Chronicle Books, 1981. The subtitle appropriately describes this as "an
intimate biography" of Steinbeck's California years by an old friend
from less prosperous days—more valuable as a repository of anecdotes
than as a source of factual data.

WATT, F. W. *John Steinbeck.* Edinburgh and London: Oliver and Boyd;
New York: Grove Press, 1962. A thin but sophisticated introduction of
Steinbeck to European readers that emphasizes his regionalism and
the effect of "nonteleological thinking" on his fiction.

2. Symposia Devoted to Steinbeck Biography and Criticism

ASTRO, RICHARD, and TETSUMARO HAYASHI, eds. *Steinbeck: The Man and
His Work.* Corvallis: Oregon State University Press, 1971. Collects ten
biographical and critical articles based on papers delivered at a Steinbeck conference at Oregon State University in 1970.

DAVIS, ROBERT MURRAY, ed. *Steinbeck: A Collection of Critical Essays.*
Twentieth Century Views Series. Englewood Cliffs, N.J.: Prentice-
Hall, 1972. Reprints a dozen essays by the best known of the early
commentators on Steinbeck's fiction.

FRENCH, WARREN, ed. *A Companion to "The Grapes of Wrath."* New
York: Viking Press, 1963. Reprints *Their Blood Is Strong,* Steinbeck's
reports on the migrants from the *San Francisco News,* along with material on the historical background of the novel and critical responses
to it.

HAYASHI, TETSUMARO, ed. Several volumes of the Steinbeck Monograph Series (Muncie, Ind.: John Steinbeck Society of America, various dates) collect articles from the *Steinbeck Quarterly,* along with original commissioned essays: *Steinbeck and the Arthurian Theme,* no. 5, 1975; *Steinbeck's Women: Essays in Criticism,* no. 9, 1979; *Steinbeck's Travel Literature: Essays in Criticism,* no. 10, 1980.

————. *Steinbeck's Literary Dimension: A Guide to Comparative Studies.* Metuchen, N.J.: Scarecrow Press, 1973. A collection of eleven essays by various writers comparing Steinbeck with Dickens, Faulkner, Hemingway, Kazantzakis, D. H. Lawrence, Daniel Mainwaring, John Milton, J. D. Salinger, Adlai Stevenson, Robert Penn Warren, and Emile Zola, accompanied by reviews of scholarship by Peter Lisca and the editor.

————. *A Study Guide to Steinbeck,* Parts I and II. Metuchen, N.J.: Scarecrow Press, 1974, 1979. Original critical discussion of Steinbeck's novels and nonfictional works by various authors, with suggestions for their use in classrooms.

————. *A Study Guide to Steinbeck's "The Long Valley."* Ann Arbor: Pierian Press, 1976. Essays by different authors on each of the stories in Steinbeck's only collection.

HAYASHI, TETSUMARO, YASUO HASHIGUCHI, and RICHARD F. PETERSEN, eds. *John Steinbeck: East and West.* Steinbeck Monograph Series, no. 8. Muncie, Ind.: John Steinbeck Society of America, 1978. A report of the proceedings of the First International John Steinbeck Congress, held in Japan in 1977, reprinting major papers delivered by Japanese and American scholars.

HAYASHI, TETSUMARO, and KENNETH D. SWAN, eds. *Steinbeck's Prophetic Vision of America.* Muncie, Ind.: John Steinbeck Society of America, 1976. Collects the papers delivered at a symposium at Taylor University to celebrate during the Bicentennial year Steinbeck's contributions to American literature.

LISCA, PETER, ed. *"The Grapes of Wrath": Text and Criticism.* New York: Viking Press, 1972. A complete resetting of the text of the novel, accompanied by some previously unpublished Steinbeck letters and critical discussions of the novel by several writers.

SAN JOSE STUDIES, November 1975. A special "John Steinbeck Issue" of this periodical, edited at San Jose State University by Martha Heasley Cox, containing original biographical and critical articles about the novelist.

Steinbeck Quarterly. Begun as the *Steinbeck Newsletter* in 1968, but issued under the present title since vol. 2 in 1969 by the John Steinbeck Society of America and Ball State University at Muncie, Indiana. Edited by Tetsumaro Hayashi, the journal is a repository of critical articles, reviews, and biographical and bibliographical notes about Steinbeck and his work. An especially good source of information about

Steinbeck studies abroad.

TEDLOCK, ERNEST W., JR., and C. V. WICKER, eds. *Steinbeck and His Critics: A Record of Twenty-Five Years*. Albuquerque: University of New Mexico Press, 1957. The first compilation of critical articles about Steinbeck reprints many of the essays of continuing value from the 1930s and 1940s, along with Peter Lisca's survey of the scholarship predating the publication of his *The Wide World of John Steinbeck* (see citation above).

Index